APPLIED DEVELOPMENTAL SCIENCE
Volume 5, Number 3

2001

SPECIAL ISSUE:

CONDITIONS FOR OPTIMAL DEVELOPMENT IN ADOLESCENCE: AN EXPERIENTIAL APPROACH

ARTICLES

Editors   RICHARD M. LERNER, Tufts University
   CELIA B. FISHER, Fordham University
   RICHARD A. WEINBERG, University of Minnesota

Editorial Assistant   LISA MARIE DIFONZO, Tufts University

Published by Routledge
2 Park Square, Milton Park, Abingdon, Oxon OX14 4RN
711 Third Avenue, New York, NY 10017, USA

Routledge is an imprint of the Taylor & Francis Group, an informa business

Applied Developmental Science
2001, Vol. 5, No. 3, 122–124

Conditions for Optimal Development in Adolescence: An Experiential Approach

Mihaly Csikszentmihalyi
Claremont Graduate University

Barbara Schneider
University of Chicago

For the social sciences to help improve the quality of life, it is necessary for research on human behavior to move out of the confines of the laboratory and the classroom. Experimental psychology—physiological, cognitive, and social—has enriched our understanding immensely. Tens of thousands of studies using paper-and-pencil tests with high school and college students have also yielded useful information. Yet research done in such settings tells us little about the processes that take place in everyday life—the small but complex psychological changes that may result, for instance, from walking in a park, meeting a friend after being alone, or watching TV after studying. Without an understanding of the phenomenology of everyday life, the human sciences lack a vital ingredient.

About 30 years ago, Csikszentmihalyi and a group of graduate students at the University of Chicago started an effort to develop a systematic phenomenology—a method that would make it possible to get reliable quantitative measures of the variation in experiential states as a person moved from morning to night in the daily round of activities. This eventually resulted in the Experience Sampling Method (ESM), which is basically a way to get "snapshots" of a person's consciousness at random moments of the day by having the person describe his or her physical, cognitive, emotional, and motivational states whenever a pager signals. In typical studies, respondents give 7 to 8 responses each day for a week, for a total of 35 to 56 responses. In the Alfred P. Sloan Study of Youth and Social Development, on which several of the articles in this special issue are based, respondents gave a total of more than 27,000 responses at Time 1, and a comparable number at Time 2, 2 years later.

The ESM has resulted in several books and many articles describing such issues as the effects of tele-vision viewing on a person's life (Kubey & Csikszentmihalyi, 1990), the effects of energy consumption on happiness (Graef, Gianninno, & Csikszentmihalyi, 1981), and the differing ways in which husbands and wives experience the same interaction (Larson & Richards, 1994). If the method has not become universally used, it is no doubt due in large part to the fact that it requires more logistic preparation than most social science research entails. However, the effort one must invest in ESM research is paid back by the richness of the data it provides. An ESM database is like a virtual laboratory to which one can return time and time again, asking new questions and performing new analyses to obtain fresh answers without having to collect new data. The fact that in the long run it saves time and resources is only one of the advantages of the ESM. Although noting that the ESM, like other methodologies, has limitations, critics agree that this method "is useful in assessing human behavior and subjective emotional states and in understanding interpersonal relationships" (National Research Council, 2000, p. 42).

For the past decade, we have been using the ESM to study adolescent development (Csikszentmihalyi & Schneider, 2000; Schneider & Stevenson, 1999), and more recently to examine life in working families. The ESM in conjunction with other methods has provided us with a window into the psychological states and contexts that affect individual and family well-being. In this special issue, we present five articles that use the ESM to illustrate various possible applications of the method for studying both adolescents and families. Each study is quite different in the questions it addresses, but they all focus on adolescent development and, with the exception of Larson, Dworkin, and Gillman's (this issue) study, all use the same longitudinal sample of more than 800 adolescents who participated in the Alfred P. Sloan Study of Youth and Social Development. Although quite different in their approaches, these studies implicitly share a general set of assumptions. They look at development as a self-organizing process (e.g., Csikszentmihalyi & Rathunde, 1998; Deci & Ryan, 1985; Lerner, 1998) during which

---

We thank Lisa Hoogstra, a graduate student in human development at the University of Chicago, who served as editorial assistant for this special issue. Of course, our deepest thanks go to Richard Lerner who invited us to edit this special issue.

Requests for reprints should be sent to Barbara Schneider, University of Chicago, 1155 East 60th Street, Chicago, IL 60637. E-mail: schneidr@norcmail.uchicago.edu

persons make choices motivated in part by the experiences that follow on their actions (Csikszentmihalyi & Massimini, 1985). If a child is bored by reading, it is unlikely that he or she will read much as an adult. A teenager who feels excited and happy only when hanging out with friends or when partying is unlikely to develop adult skills that require long hours of study and self-discipline. Thus, the quality of experience teenagers report gives a clue as to the kind of adults they are going to become.

The first article by Moneta, Schneider, and Csikszentmihalyi (this issue) employs multilevel models to address an old developmental question: How real is the *Sturm und Drang* of the teenage years? The study shows that the answer to this question is more complex than it is usually thought to be. Variables measuring self-esteem and locus of control show a steady linear improvement over the teenage years. Items measuring self-worth (e.g., living up to one's expectations and feeling successful) indicate a clear concave-up trend, bottoming at ages 15 and 16. In other words, sixth-grade children start out with strongly positive feelings about self, but by eighth grade these feelings are less positive. They fall further by 10th grade and start moving upward again after that. Finally, variables measuring affective states (e.g., feeling good and feeling happy) follow a downward trend that does not show improvement by Grade 12.

The study also uncovers several variations around this basic trend. For instance, children of different ethnic groups and those from traditional versus single-parent and reconstituted families follow different experiential curves in their development. However, even within groups that exhibited less positive developmental trajectories, the effects were not uniform across different personality and experiential measures, nor were they permanent across adolescence. Moneta et al.'s findings suggest that the turmoil associated with adolescence may be overstated because it appears to vary across different measures and contexts.

The second article by Larson et al. (this issue) addresses how single-parent families help their children use time more constructively. As the number of children growing up in nontraditional families is approaching parity with those in traditional families, this question is becoming increasingly relevant for the well-being of families. Larson et al. found that single parenthood is not inevitably a hardship. Single-parent families that function well (i.e., that exercise firm parental control and establish family routines) have children who use their free time constructively. Mother's employment does not appear to affect children's use of time; rather, it is how mothers spend their free time. Mothers who read, attend religious services, or are involved in other constructive activities are likely to have children who engage in these activities.

In the next article, Rathunde (this issue) looks more closely at the effects of particular family processes on the development of optimal patterns of attention in children. Taking a cue from James (1890), Rathunde argues that an essential task for each person is to develop "undivided attention," or the ability to get involved with everyday tasks in a way that is enjoyable and productive at the same time. In a longitudinal analysis, Rathunde finds that, over time, children who see their families as providing both challenge (i.e., expectations and opportunities for expressing individual excellence) and support (i.e., a context of warmth and caring) spend more of their day in conditions of undivided attention. Those whose families are only challenging are more likely to experience drudgery, and those who are only supported typically spend more time "fooling"—that is, more time on activities that are enjoyable but not productive. Rathunde's findings point to the need for a balance between family challenge and support in helping adolescents realize their capacity for self-regulation and lifelong learning.

The next article by Hektner (this issue) draws on several of the same themes as the two previous ones. He uses structural equation modeling to estimate relationships between family and school contexts, individual characteristics, and subjective experiences. Hektner shows that growth-conducive experience (i.e., responses that indicate a person experiences intrinsic motivation, concentration, and goal-directedness while engaged in productive activities) remains quite stable as an individual trait over a 2-year period, although it does increase overall with time. Several environmental conditions show a strong relation with growth-conducive experiences when the two are measured at the same time, and the effects are still strong, directly or mediated through experience at Time 1 in a longitudinal analysis. Hektner's analysis points to the importance of conducive environments both in the family and at school for promoting optimal development in adolescence.

The study by Asakawa (this issue) focuses on whether different ethnic groups experience life in different ways, and more specifically, whether Asian American adolescents report the same quality of experience as White adolescents when involved in studying and other productive activities. Asakawa shows that although both ethnic groups feel worse than usual when studying, the drop in quality of experience is greater for Whites. He believes that this is in part due to the fact that Asian American parents expect high academic achievement from their children, but leave them largely free to implement their academic goals. White parents, by contrast, expect less in the long run, but micromanage their children's education. This elegant comparison shows how the ESM may be used to perform research that illuminates the inner experiences of people from very different cultural contexts, in a way that makes rigorous quantitative comparisons possible.

The articles included in this special issue contribute to the fund of information necessary to understand what enables young people to become self-directed, autonomous individuals in control of their own destinies. Perhaps their strength lies in their identification of parenting practices that promote adolescent well-being. Too often, parents assume that their parenting role ceases when their children learn to drive and that their primary responsibility in high school and later is helping their children select and pay for college. These articles open new conceptual areas for the study of family and school contexts and their influence on adolescent development.

References

Csikszentmihalyi, M., & Massimini, F. (1985). On the psychological selection of bio-cultural information. *New Ideas in Psychology, 3*(2), 115–138.

Csikszentmihalyi, M., & Rathunde, K. (1998). The development of the person: An experiential perspective on the ontogenesis of psychological complexity. In W. Damon (Ed.-in-Chief) & R. M. Lerner (Vol. Ed.), *Handbook of child psychology (5th ed.): Vol. 1. Theoretical models of human development* (pp. 635–684). New York: Wiley.

Csikszentmihalyi, M., & Schneider, B. (2000). *Becoming adult: How teenagers prepare for the world of work.* New York: Basic Books.

Deci, E. L., & Ryan, R. M. (1985). *Intrinsic motivation and self-determination in human behavior.* New York: Plenum.

Graef, R., Gianninno, S., & Csikszentmihalyi, M. (1981). Energy consumption in leisure and perceived happiness. In J. D. Claxton, C. D. Anderson, J. R. Brent Richie, & G. McDougall (Eds.), *Consumer and energy consumption: International perspectives on research and policy options* (pp. 47–55). New York: Praeger.

James, W. (1890). *The principles of psychology.* New York: Dover.

Kubey, R., & Csikszentmihalyi, M. (1990). *Television and the quality of life: How viewing shapes everyday experience.* Hillsdale, NJ: Lawrence Erlbaum Associates, Inc.

Larson, R., & Richards, M. (1994). *Divergent realities: The emotional lives of mothers, fathers, and adolescents.* New York: Basic Books.

Lerner, R. M. (1998). Theories of human development: Contemporary perspectives. In W. Damon (Ed.-in-Chief) & R. M. Lerner (Vol. Ed.), *Handbook of child psychology (5th ed.): Vol. 1. Theoretical models of human development* (pp. 1–24). New York: Wiley.

National Research Council. (2000). *Time use measurement and research: Report of a workshop.* Washington, DC: National Academy Press.

Schneider, B., & Stevenson, D. (1999). *The ambitious generation: America's teenagers motivated but directionless.* New Haven, CT: Yale University Press.

Applied Developmental Science
2001, Vol. 5, No. 3, 125–142

A Longitudinal Study of the Self-Concept and Experiential Components of Self-Worth and Affect Across Adolescence

Giovanni B. Moneta
The Chinese University of Hong Kong

Barbara Schneider
University of Chicago

Mihaly Csikszentmihalyi
Claremont Graduate University

Classic theories depict adolescence as a period of emotional "storm and stress." Empirical evidence, mostly from cross-sectional studies, suggests that emotional development presents a mixture of continuity, swings, and resilience. We examined longitudinally the average grade trends in components of self-concept and experiential components of self-worth and affect across adolescence. We followed 1,165 6th through 12th graders for 4 years using a 3-wave, accelerated longitudinal design. Participants completed self-concept scales (global self-esteem and locus of control), and the Experience Sampling Method, which provided daily self-reports on self-worth (living up to one's own expectations, to the expectations of others, feeling successful, and feeling in control of the situation) and affect (feeling good about oneself and feeling happy). Multilevel modeling indicated that both self-esteem and locus of control grow linearly over time. Self-worth components of experience showed a concave-up trend bottoming around Grade 10, suggesting a pubertal swing and partial readjustment by the end of adolescence. Affect declined quadratically across adolescence. Compared to White students, less positive grade trends were found for Hispanics, Asian Americans, and adolescents from nontraditional families. A mixed pattern emerged for African Americans. Behind the stable growth of components of self-concept, adolescents experience a certain degree of discontinuity as to how they evaluate their capability to meet everyday life demands and their affect declines. The modifications in grade trends due to ethnicity and family structure call for studies on the possible influence exercised by family processes and school environments.

Almost a century ago, Hall (1904) introduced a view of adolescence as a period of "storm and stress" characterized by three key features: mood disruptions, conflicts with parents, and risk behaviors. Although these emotional and behavioral responses can occur at any point in a person's life, Hall believed that they are far more common among adolescents and are largely endogenous, determined by biological factors associated with pubertal development. However, Hall recognized that the extent to which adolescents produce the storm-and-stress pattern depends on their temperament and the culture in which they live. He claimed that adolescence was less disruptive in cultures characterized by conservative traditions, and identified urbanization as the key factor. In his view, urbanization implies

greater temptations to vice and reduced opportunities for physical activity and exploration, which he regarded as an inherent and biological need of adolescents. Thus, he claimed that many of the problems of adolescence were produced by the social inability to understand its nature and risks and to adapt the social institutions accordingly.

In the following decades, classic theories of personality development have contributed to the understanding of the emotional disruptions of adolescence. S. Freud (1910) stated that the emotional turmoil of adolescence stems from the awakening of the sexual instinct. Adolescence corresponds to the genital psychosexual developmental stage that follows the latency stage. The latency stage is a long and seemingly quiet period during which the libido expresses itself only indirectly through playing, schooling, and socializing, and the child loses all curiosity and interest in sex. By contrast, the genital stage is the period in which the sexual drive returns and transforms itself into a ma-

Requests for reprints should be sent to Giovanni B. Moneta, The Chinese University of Hong Kong, Department of Psychology, Shatin, New Territories, Hong Kong. E-mail: gbmoneta@hotmail.com

ture form, and adolescents face increasing societal demands to develop their intellectual and practical abilities. Thus, Freud explained the emotional disruptions of adolescence as the result of the conflict between instinctual strivings and reality demands. Within the psychoanalytic tradition, A. Freud (1946, 1958) argued that puberty implies abrupt increases of libidinal energy. At the same time, socialization leads to the development of a more demanding superego. These two simultaneous processes modify the power relation between psychological structures, reducing balance and stability, and increasing the intensity and frequency of emotional disruptions. She viewed this process as universal and argued that the absence of emotional disruptions during adolescence reflects excessive defenses and is therefore pathological.

Ego psychologists departed from Freud's theory by reducing the importance attributed to the sexual instinct and attributing greater importance to the pleasure derived from mastering tasks, ego development, and social influence. Within Erikson's (1968) paradigm, adolescence encompasses two psychosocial crises: industry versus inferiority and identity versus role confusion. The onset of the first crisis coincides with schooling age, and the crisis ends during puberty. The onset of the second crisis coincides with the midpoint of adolescence, and the crisis may continue through young adulthood. Thus, Erikson explained the emotional disruptions of adolescence as the result of two strivings: (a) developing competence and proving it to oneself and others, and (b) developing a sense of identity that satisfies one's need to be unique while obtaining social acceptance and recognition. Research by Marcia (1966, 1980) has proven that not all adolescents experience an identity crisis. Some have not thought of identity issues and have not charted directions in life, and thus remain in a state of identity diffusion. Others have chosen an identity suggested by significant others without constructing it by raising questions and seeking answers, and they are thus in a state of foreclosure. These findings suggest that the emotional disruptions of adolescence that may arise from an identity crisis are more likely among adolescents than adults, but are neither universal nor necessary.

The theories of Hall, Freud, and Erikson have profoundly influenced empirical research on adolescence in the past decades. In a review of the literature on the storm and stress of adolescence, Arnett (1999) concluded that the collected evidence supports the existence of all the hallmarks of adolescence: mood disruptions, conflicts with parents, and risk behaviors. However, not all adolescents experience this triad, and there are large individual differences in the extent to which adolescents experience each of the three components. From the cultural point of view, he argued that storm and stress are lower or even absent in traditional cultures that promote a *narrow socialization*—that is,

that impose a narrower range on the development of individual differences and put lesser emphasis on individualism (Arnett, 1995). He also suggested that storm and stress may be reduced within the North American minority cultures. Thus, Arnett proposed a modified storm-and-stress view that allows for wide individual and cultural differences, wherein the key cultural component is not urbanization but breadth of socialization and emphasis on individualism.

This study focuses on the issue of the emotional disruptions of adolescence. A large body of research has tried to answer the basic question of whether emotions are less stable in adolescence than in other periods of life. Emotions have been assessed by paper-and-pencil, one-point-in-time measures and by paper-and-pencil, time-contingent sampling measures of experience in daily life (Wheeler & Reis, 1991) such as the Experience Sampling Method (ESM; Csikszentmihalyi & Larson, 1987; Csikszentmihalyi, Larson, & Prescott, 1977). Whereas the first group of techniques is designed to measure relatively stable, person-specific emotional tendencies, the second group of techniques is designed to assess the moment-to-moment, situation-to-situation variations in activity and experience, making it possible to investigate the development of adolescents' interactions with their environment.

Research conducted by either type of technique has provided inconsistent evidence on how stable emotions are across adolescence. Some findings suggest that emotions are as stable (or unstable) during adolescence as they are during the course of adult life (Block, 1971; Davis & Franzoi, 1991; Rutter, Graham, Chadwick, & Yule, 1976; Steinberg, 1990). Other findings suggest that adolescence features far greater swings of emotions (Larson, Csikszentmihalyi, & Graef, 1980) and decreasing trends from early to late adolescence (Csikszentmihalyi & Larson, 1984; Larson & Lampman-Petraitis, 1989). Thus, the dilemma concerning the emotional disruptions of adolescence is still unsolved.

There are two possible reasons for this stalemate. First, most studies conducted to date are cross-sectional (e.g., Csikszentmihalyi & Larson, 1984; Larson & Lampman-Petraitis, 1989) and thus are potentially influenced by cohort effects. If the storm and stress of adolescence is modified by unknown societal changes, then cross-sectional comparisons between adolescents of different age groups are confounded by the unknown variables. From this perspective, the issue of stability can be studied best as an issue of individual change within a longitudinal study. Second, the two types of measures (traditional and experiential) have rarely been used together on the same study population, and thus, differences between the dispositional and experiential realities of emotions could not be compared. It is likely that dispositional measures imply more cognitive processing, comparative judgments, and rationalizations than experiential, in situ measures that are collected on a hourly basis. If that is the case, the two sets of measures could produce different answers to the research question. From this perspective, the issue of stability can be studied best using a multimethod approach.

An interesting longitudinal study (Larson, Richards, Moneta, Holmbeck, & Duckett, 1996) investigated the average age trend of the experience of affect during familial interactions in a large sample of adolescents from White, middle-class families. Daily affect was operationalized as the mean of three experiential variables: feeling happy–unhappy, cheerful–irritable, and friendly–angry. The analysis focused only on those observations that were collected while the adolescents were interacting with their families. Findings indicated that the sample mean of affect with family decreases from early adolescence and increases by late adolescence, returning to virtually the same level. This concave-up age trend was more marked and lasted longer for girls. Based on the analysis of the content of familial interactions (e.g., talking vs. being in the same environment with no communication), the authors interpreted this swing in affect as the result of a process of disengagement from family and transformation of family relationships toward a more egalitarian model. The emerging pattern disconfirms the common belief that adolescence is a period of sharp conflicts with family, and suggests that adolescence is a phase of progressive transformations rather than crises.

This study builds on Larson and colleagues' (1996) approach to investigate the presence or absence of the storm and stress of adolescence in a large, representative sample of U.S. teenagers followed longitudinally for 4 years. We envision the research problem as a study of continuity versus discontinuity of development—that is, as constancy (or lack of constancy) of group means across age (e.g., McCall, 1977; Moss & Susman, 1980). We investigate average age trends in two dispositional variables, assessed by one-point-in-time surveys, and six experiential variables, assessed by the ESM. The dispositional variables are basic components of the self-concept: global self-esteem (Coopersmith, 1967; Rosenberg, 1979) and locus of control (Rotter, 1966). Four experiential variables measure self-worth in daily activities: living up to one's own expectations, living up to the expectations of others, feeling successful, and feeling in control. The remaining two experiential variables measure affect in daily activities: feeling good about oneself and feeling happy. These variables are selected to cover a wide range of adolescents' self-perceptions that may reflect the presence, absence, and intensity of storm and stress.

For each of these variables, we model the average developmental trajectory starting from early adolescence (approximately age 12) and ending with late adolescence (approximately age 18). Evidence in favor of or against the storm-and-stress view is evaluated for each variable separately by examining whether the mean developmental trajectory reveals continuity or discontinuity: Discontinuity supports the presence of storm and stress, and continuity disconfirms it. We consider two basic patterns of continuity: lack of change and progressive linear change. The first pattern is the absolute continuity; the second implies a smooth buildup of self-perceptions. We consider two basic patterns of discontinuity: a concave-up trend with a minimum within adolescence, and a concave-up trend with an estimated minimum projected beyond adolescence. The first pattern is a swing leading to partial or total recovery by late adolescence; the second implies an accelerated decrease with no recovery.

This study has two goals. The first goal is to provide a comprehensive description of continuity and discontinuity across adolescence. Based on this set of analyses, we aim to clarify two complementary issues: (a) whether the development of self-concept, experiential self-worth, and affect variables is continuous (and thus inconsistent with the storm-and-stress view) or discontinuous (and thus consistent with the storm-and-stress view), and (b) whether the several dispositional and experiential variables provide a consistent pattern (i.e., they all exhibit either continuity or discontinuity) or a diversified, more complex pattern (i.e., some exhibit continuity and others discontinuity).

Based on previous theoretical and empirical research, we formulate the following hypotheses. The ego psychologists (Block, 1993; Block & Block, 1980; Funder & Block, 1989; Loevinger, 1976, 1985, 1993; White, 1959, 1960, 1963) highlight the child's or adolescent's natural tendency to develop a firm sense of self, the ability to cope with stress, the ability to delay gratification for achieving distal goals, and the ability to establish and deepen relationships. Although the nomological network is complex, measures of the ego appear to be related to measures of self-esteem and locus of control. For example, Deci and Ryan (1985a, 1985b) found that ego development (Loevinger, 1976) correlates positively with the autonomy causality orientation, representing a person's tendency toward self-determination, and negatively with the impersonal causality orientation, representing a person's lack of motivational structures supporting either self-determined or controlled behavior. In turn, the autonomy orientation correlates positively with self-esteem, whereas the impersonal orientation correlates negatively with self-esteem and positively with external locus of control. This body of research leads us to believe that the two investigated components of the self-concept (global self-esteem and locus of control) are related to ego development, and thus should exhibit substantial continuity across adolescence. On the other hand, Larson and colleagues' (1996) findings on the daily experience of affect lead us to believe that feeling happy and good should be discontinuous, exhibiting a swing with a low in midadolescence and possibly a recovery afterward. Concerning the experiential variables measuring self-worth (feeling successful, in control, and living up to one's and others' expectations), we cannot commit ourselves to specific hypotheses. Although one might expect these variables to be related to global self-esteem and locus of control, these relations do not guarantee that their developmental trajectories are similar.

The second goal is to shed light on whether the mean developmental trajectories in self-concept, experiential self-worth, and affect variables are modified by gender, ethnicity, and family structure. Based on this second group of analyses, we aim to clarify whether adolescents from disadvantaged groups show natural resilience and ability to recover from swings in self-perception by the end of adolescence.

This second part of the analysis is largely exploratory. Numerous cross-sectional studies have made comparisons by gender and ethnic group, and provided somewhat complex evidence indicating that women and minority groups have lower self-esteem and a more external locus of control (e.g., Gaa & Shores, 1979; Hughes & Demo, 1989; Kling, Hyde, Showers, & Buswell, 1999; Wylie, 1979). Yet, no study has performed longitudinal comparisons of average developmental trajectories. Furthermore, with some exceptions (e.g., Asakawa & Csikszentmihalyi, 1998), previous studies of daily subjective experience have not focused on differences between the North American cultural majority and minorities.

Methods

Participants

Participants were the 1,309 members of the Alfred P. Sloan Study of Youth and Social Development who were followed longitudinally for 4 years. Participants were recruited following a nationwide random sampling scheme. The gender distribution of the sample was 586 (44.8%) boys and 723 (55.2%) girls. The ethnic distribution was 720 (55.0%) Whites, 205 (15.6%) Hispanics, 288 (22.0%) African Americans, 82 (6.3%) Asian Americans, 12 (.9%) Native Americans, and 2 participants of unknown ethnicity.

Data collection proceeded in three waves (1992–1993, 1994–1995, and 1996–1997) according to an accelerated longitudinal study design. The starting sample comprised 1,109 middle school and high school students from Grades 6, 8, 10, and 12, corresponding approximately to ages 12, 14, 16, and 18 years. Additional participants were recruited in the second and third waves. A total of 171 (13.1%) participants completed all three data collection waves, 374

(28.5%) completed two waves, and 764 (58.3%) completed only one wave. The grade distribution by wave is shown in Table 1.

Measures

In each wave of data collection, participants were administered the Teenage Life Questionnaire (TLQ; Csikszentmihalyi & Schneider, 2000) and the ESM (see Csikszentmihalyi & Larson, 1987, and Csikszentmihalyi et al., 1977, regarding construction of the ESM). The adolescents' quality of daily experience was studied using the ESM. Each participant was given a programmable wristwatch and a block of identical response forms to carry for 7 consecutive days. The wristwatch was programmed to signal eight times a day at random intervals from 7:30 a.m. to 10:30 p.m. Participants were instructed to complete a response form immediately after each signal. The form contained open-ended questions for identifying the activity and its context, and scaled items for measuring a wide range of feelings associated with the activity.

In this study we employed three sets of questions from the TLQ: (a) questions concerning family composition and structure, (b) a global self-esteem scale, and (c) a locus of control scale. Participant's family structure was evaluated based only on responses obtained during the first wave of data collection. The family structure distribution was 707 (53.8%) from traditional families, 243 (18.8%) from single-parent families, 175 (13.3%) from reconstituted families, 42 (3.2%) from other types of families, and 142 (10.8%) of unknown family structure.

Global self-esteem was assessed by a 7-item abridged version of Rosenberg's (1979) Self-Esteem Scale. Locus of control was assessed by a 6-item abridged version of Rotter's (1966) Locus of Control Scale. All items were rated on a 4-point scale ranging from 1 (*strongly disagree*) to 4 (*strongly agree*). Scores for each participant were computed by averaging the respective items. In cases of nonresponse, the individual score was computed over the available

Table 1. *Participants' Grade Distribution by Data Collection Waves*

Data Collection Wave	Grade in School						
	6	7	8	9	10	11	12
1st (1992–1993)	303	—	312	—	262	—	232
2nd (1994–1995)	—	—	215	—	190	—	187
3rd (1996–1997)	—	—	—	—	162	—	164

Note: Distributions refer to 1,309 participants; 171 contributed to all three waves of data collection, 374 to two, and 764 to one. No data collection occurred when students were in 7th, 9th, or 11th grades.

items. High values mean high self-esteem and internal locus of control, respectively.

Six scaled variables from the ESM were used. Four variables measured time-contingent self-worth: Were you living up to your own expectations, Were you living up to expectations of others, Were you succeeding at what you were doing, and Did you feel in control of the situation. The remaining two variables measured time-contingent affect: Did you feel good about yourself, and the semantic differential scale sad–happy. The Sad–Happy scale was scored from 1 to 7; the other five variables were scored from 1 to 9, with 1 being the most negative and 9 the most positive value.

Selections, data structures, and missing data.

To avoid potentially confounding factors, several participants had to be removed from the analysis. We excluded all participants of unknown family structure and the 2 participants of unknown ethnicity, resulting in a sample size of 1,165.

The total number of data points available for the analysis is the sum of all repeated observations performed on each participant in the sample. The dispositional variables are one-point-in-time measures, whereas the experiential variables are repeated measures. Participants have up to three repeated measures of the dispositional variables over follow-up (i.e., one per data collection wave), and up to 168 experiential measures (i.e., 56 per data collection wave). Thus, the number of data points for the experiential variables greatly exceeded that for the dispositional variables. After elimination of missing data, the number of data points was 1,612 for global self-esteem, 1,577 for locus of control, 44,393 for living up to one's own expectations, 44,622 for living up to the expectations of others, 44,193 for feeling successful, 44,654 for feel-

ing in control, 44,725 for feeling good, and 43,183 for feeling happy.

Stability of the variables.

In all preliminary analyses conducted for evaluating the temporal stability of the variables and their interrelations, we proceeded by aggregating the data at the individual level. For each participant and wave of data collection, we computed individual means of repeated ESM measures—that is, the average value of each scale over the entire week of the ESM. We then utilized these individual means as if they were one-point-in-time test scores. After aggregation, the number of data points was 2,012 for living up to one's own expectations, 2,013 for living up to the expectations of others, 2,006 for feeling successful, 2,014 for feeling in control, 2,016 for feeling good, and 1,996 for feeling happy.

We investigated the longitudinal stability of the variables by estimating their respective test–retest correlation coefficients over waves of data collection. Table 2 shows the correlation coefficients relative to all three possible comparisons. In general, the variables show a fair stability over adolescence, indicating that the relative ranking of the individuals within the sample remains much the same over time. The dispositional variables are the most stable, followed by the experiential variable feeling good about oneself. The least stable variable is feeling happy, which shows poor correlation coefficients from the first and second wave to the last one. This finding suggests that, compared to the other variables, daily happiness in adolescence is less of a personal tendency and more of an environmental factor.

Relations between variables.

The eight dispositional and experiential variables had fair reciprocal correlations across waves of data collection. Focusing on

Table 2. *Two- and 4-year Test–Retest Correlation Coefficients Estimated by Comparing the Same Measures Across the Three Waves of Data Collection*

	Comparisons of Waves of Data Collection		
	1st vs. 2nd	2nd vs. 3rd	1st vs. 3rd
Time Lag (Years)	2	2	4
Range of n	455–493	189–199	187–194
Global Self-Esteem[a]	.63	.65	.64
Locus of Control (E–I)[a]	.62	.59	.51
Living Up to Your Own Expectations[b]	.51	.48	.38
Living Up to the Expectations of Others[b]	.50	.55	.49
Feeling Successful[b]	.54	.53	.48
Feeling in Control[b]	.43	.42	.34
Feeling Good[b]	.60	.50	.51
Sad–Happy[b]	.55	.21	.22

Note: Correlation coefficients were computed after pairwise elimination of missing data. E–I = External–Internal.
[a]Correlation coefficients refer to individual test scores. [b]Correlation coefficients refer to individual means of repeated Experience Sampling Method scores.

the first wave only, for example, the correlation between global self-esteem and locus of control (External–Internal) was .55. The highest correlation between the two dispositional variables and the six experiential variables was the one involving global self-esteem and feeling good about oneself (.46); the other correlations ranged from .20 to .31. The experiential variables correlated with each other in the range from .17 to .60.

We then examined more deeply the relations among the eight variables by conducting separate principal component analyses, with varimax rotation, for each wave of data collection. The main criterion for selecting the number of factors was to include all factors with eigenvalues greater than 1. In addition, we evaluated the sensitivity of this criterion by inspecting scree plots and assessing the presence of scales showing double loadings. For each wave, we identified three factors. As shown in Table 3, the three-factor solutions are remarkably consistent across time. The first factor included the four experiential components of self-worth and thus was named experiential self-worth. The second factor included the two dispositional variables (locus of control and self-esteem) and thus was named self-concept. The third factor included feeling happy and feeling good about oneself and thus was named affect. Feeling good about oneself had a second loading on the experiential self-worth factor; thus, this salient judgment seems to involve both the evaluation of how well one is doing and the affective response to that evaluation.

Statistical Methods

Mathematical modeling of grade trends. To investigate average grade trends in the eight selected dispositional and experiential variables, we utilized one basic mathematical model:

Dependent variable = $\beta_0 + \beta_1$ grade (linear) + β_2 grade (quadratic)

where β_0 is the grand mean (i.e., the mean expected value of the dependent variable when grade is equal to zero); grade (linear) is a numerical variable representing student's grade at the time the dependent variable was assessed, and β_1 is its mean effect on the dependent variable; grade (quadratic) is the same numerical variable raised to the second power, and β_2 is its mean effect on the dependent variable. All mean regression coefficients β_0 through β_2 have to be estimated based on the data, and may turn out to be either significantly different from or equal to zero. This simple model can adequately describe linear growth or decrease, curvilinear growth or decrease, or absence of both. For example, the hypothesis that global self-esteem grows linearly as a function of grade corresponds to the case $\beta_1 > 0$ and $\beta_2 = 0$. The hypothesis that self-esteem has a concave-up relation with grade corresponds to the case $\beta_1 < 0$ and $\beta_2 > 0$. Whether the concave-up trend ends with total, partial, or no recovery can be determined by simple computations based on the point estimates of the regression coefficients, or by plotting the predicted values over grade.

The hypothesis that adolescence implies continuity is compatible with either (a) the absence of an average linear or nonlinear grade trend, corresponding to absence of change; or (b) a positive average linear grade trend, corresponding to a smooth and progressive buildup throughout adolescence. The hypothesis that adolescence implies discontinuity is compatible with three average grade trends: (a) a negative linear trend,

Table 3. *Factor Loadings of the Measures of the Self-Concept, Experiential Self-Worth, and Affect for Each Wave of Data Collection*

	Data Collection Waves								
	1st (1992–1993) Factors			2nd (1994–1995) Factors			3rd (1996–1997) Factors		
Measures	I	II	III	I	II	III	I	II	III
Living Up to Your Own Expectations[a]	.885	.125	.161	.872	.172	.200	.827	.179	.189
Living Up to the Expectations of Others[a]	.842	.135	−.078	.828	.121	−.061	.806	.163	−.176
Feeling Successful[a]	.736	.073	.262	.780	.122	.130	.692	.113	.227
Feeling in Control[a]	.689	.086	.366	.776	.126	.310	.625	.028	.532
Locus of Control (E–I)[b]	.137	.899	−.027	.179	.898	−.049	.180	.901	.058
Global Self-Esteem[b]	.112	.812	.329	.142	.844	.295	.144	.848	.284
Sad–Happy[a]	.112	.010	.877	.085	.069	.919	−.067	.190	.806
Feeling Good[a]	.540	.254	.622	.558	.256	.629	.427	.168	.763
Explained Variance	74.2%			77.2%			73.0%		
Number of Participants	836			448			269		

Note: Factors were extracted by the method of principal components, subjected to varimax rotation, and named as experiential self-worth (I), self-concept (II), and affect (III). E–I = External–Internal.
[a]The analysis of these variables was performed on individual means of repeated Experience Sampling Method scores. [b]The analysis of these variables was performed on individual test scores.

corresponding to a smooth and progressive decrease throughout adolescence; (b) a concave-up trend indicating an accelerated decrease throughout adolescence (if the estimated minimum falls beyond Grade 12); and (c) a concave-up trend indicating a swing (if the estimated minimum falls in the 6th- to 12th-grade range) with the minimum representing a critical point of adolescence. Furthermore, concave-down trends, although unlikely, would also suggest discontinuity indicating a boosting effect (e.g., a pubertal one). We conducted the hypothesis testing on each dependent variable separately to allow us to assess the continuity and discontinuity separately for each dispositional and experiential variable.

The same mathematical model was extended to account for possible modifications of average grade trends due to gender, family structure, and ethnicity, by adding new predictors together with their interactions involving the grade terms. For example, gender modification was tested by adding the gender main effect and the interactions of gender with grade to the initial model, which resulted in the following model:

Dependent variable = $\beta_0 + \beta_1$ grade (linear) + β_2 grade (quadratic) + β_3 gender + β_4 gender * grade (linear) + β_5 gender * grade (quadratic)

where gender was coded as 0 for male and 1 for female. The introduction of the new terms modifies the meaning of the terms that were already included in the model. Within this model, males constitute the referent group and females the contrast group. The coefficients β_0, β_1, and β_2 represent the mean grade trend for adolescent boys. The coefficients β_3, β_4, and β_5 represent the mean deviation (i.e., algebraic difference) from the mean grade trend due to being female—that is, the mean difference in grade trend between adolescent girls and boys. Thus, assuming that all coefficients β_0 through β_5 are statistically significant, the interpretation of the grade trend and its modification due to gender can be easily worked out by using the regression equation to compute and plot the distinct developmental trajectories for male and female adolescents. The specific pattern of statistical significance involving the coefficients β_3 through β_5 determines the presence or absence, as well as complexity level, of the modification due to gender. Three main cases should be considered. If all coefficients β_3 through β_5 are nonsignificant, then there is no modification due to gender; that is, adolescent boys and girls have the same developmental trajectory. If β_3 is significantly different from zero and β_4 and β_5 are not, then the mean trajectory for adolescent girls is parallel to that of adolescent boys. If instead coefficients β_3 through β_5 are all significantly different from zero, then the mean trajectory for adolescent girls differs from, and is not parallel to, that for adolescent boys. All other intermediate cases can be interpreted easily by inspecting the graphs of predicted values of the dependent variable over grade.

It is important to point out that by introducing simultaneously main class effects and interactions with grade or gender, family structure, and ethnicity, one automatically identifies a global referent group. In all analyses, the referent groups for family structure and ethnicity were traditional and White, respectively; thus, the global referent group was a White adolescent boy from a traditional family. By fitting the full model, the terms β_0 through β_2 define the mean trend of the dependent variable for the global referent group, and all other terms define the mean deviation from that trend due to gender, family structure, and ethnicity. By removing terms from the full model, the referent group changes. Therefore, the correct interpretation of a final model, obtained after the elimination of nonsignificant terms, requires a careful identification of the referent group.

Multilevel modeling. We estimated the coefficients of the mathematical model by multilevel modeling (Bryk & Raudenbush, 1992; Goldstein, 1987, 1995; Longford, 1993). Multilevel models are particularly useful to control for the within-subjects correlation of repeated measures, as well as for the presence of missing data. These techniques are regression procedures for modeling data with hierarchical structures. In the case of repeated measures, the data structure typically has two levels: Individuals are modeled at Level 2, and the single observations performed on them are modeled at Level 1. The modeling proceeds by fitting separate regressions for each individual to obtain an average regression model valid for the entire population from which the individuals were sampled. The estimation procedure is iterative and at each step it provides improved estimates of both person-specific and population-average regression coefficients until convergence is achieved. The person-specific coefficients and the population-average coefficients are reciprocally adjusted. Multilevel models can handle unbalanced and incomplete streams of repeated measures because the lack of information in any given individual data distribution is counterbalanced by importing information from the population average model.

The multilevel modeling of grade trends conducted in this article represents an extension of previous applications to the longitudinal modeling of time trends in sleep disorders (Moneta, Leclerc, Chastang, Dang Tran, & Goldberg, 1996) and grade trends in affect (Larson et al., 1996). For extensive presentations on how multilevel models can control for the structural complexity of the ESM data, see Moneta and Csikszentmihalyi (1996, 1999). In what follows, we focus on the specific characteristics of the application used here.

The multilevel models of the dispositional variables were fitted on the repeated test scores, and the multilevel models of the experiential variables were fitted on the much larger number of repeated, beep-level ESM measures. The number of repeated measures per participant is the main limiting factor in the number of random coefficients that can be estimated. Due to this structural difference of the data, the model for dispositional variables contained only one random coefficient, the intercept β_0, whereas the model for experiential variables contained two random coefficients, the intercept β_0 and the slope β_1 of grade (linear).

For each dependent variable separately, we first fitted the basic model containing only the intercept and the linear and quadratic effects of grade. This model allowed testing for the presence or absence of a mean grade trend relative to all participants in the sample. We then fitted the full model containing, in addition to the predictors of the basic model, all potential modifiers in the form of main class effects and their interactions with the linear and quadratic effects of grade. Lastly, by backward elimination, we selected a final model. In the selection we followed the hierarchical principle that a lower order term cannot be removed if a higher order term containing it is significant. The criterion for excluding an effect was a significance level greater than .05. The significance level was evaluated by the likelihood test. We estimated the models by means of the program ML3 (Prosser, Rasbash, & Goldstein, 1991).

The multilevel models were fitted on the full body of data, including participants from all three waves of data collection and all available repeated observations. Given that the study adopted an accelerated longitudinal design, this implies that the grade trends were estimated by pooling together complete longitudinal data (i.e., from all 171 participants who were assessed in all three waves), incomplete longitudinal data (i.e., from all participants who were assessed in two waves only), and cross-sectional data (i.e., from participants who were assessed in one wave only). Thus, the data set was structured in three cohorts (identified by the date of the first assessment) where each one of them was subject to attrition. This pooling procedure is open to two potential sources of bias: attrition effects and Grade × Cohort interaction effects (Cook & Campbell, 1979).

Attrition effects are present if the probability of dropping out of the study is associated with the dependent variable and the predictors. We ruled out this possibility by fitting the final models on the restricted sample of participants with complete longitudinal data and finding no marked differences in the point estimates of the average regression coefficients. Thus, for this data set, the pooling procedure has the advantage of providing greater statistical power without introducing a noticeable bias.

Cohort effects are present if the three cohorts differ in unmeasured background variables that influence the grade trends. We assessed the presence and size of cohort effects by the method proposed by Raudenbush and others (Miyazaki & Raudenbush, 1999; Raudenbush & Chan, 1993). Two indicator variables were created for identifying each contrast between the first cohort (1992–1993) and the other two cohorts. These indicators were then included in the Level 2 model as fixed-effects predictors. For all eight dependent variables, the cohort indicators in the basic model (containing only the linear and quadratic grade effects) turned out to be nonsignificant. These results indicate that the cohort effects were either absent or minimal and, thus, that the average grade trends were virtually identical across cohorts. Consequently, we proceeded to the estimation of all the models without including the cohort parameters.

Results

Basic Test of Grade Trends

Table 4 shows the estimated average population coefficients and variance components, with standard errors, of the basic multilevel models used to test linear and quadratic grade trends of the self-concept, experiential self-worth, and affect variables.

Both linear and quadratic grade terms for global self-esteem were nonsignificant; yet, when the quadratic effect of grade was removed, the linear trend became significantly positive ($\beta = .018$, $SE = .006$). The findings imply that, on average, global self-esteem grows linearly throughout adolescence. The estimation algorithm failed to converge for locus of control. Subsequent analyses performed by adding extra terms confirmed that the cause of the problem was that the estimate of the quadratic effect was close to zero. By removing the quadratic effect, the estimation algorithm converged and the linear grade term was significantly positive. Thus, there is a mean linear trend for locus of control to become more internal from the onset to the end of adolescence. In sum, both components of the self-concept exhibit continuity in the form of a smooth, progressive buildup.

Both linear and quadratic grade terms were significant for three of the four experiential self-worth variables (living up to one's own expectations, to the expectations of others, and feeling successful). However, both grade terms were nonsignificant for feeling in control. Refitting the model by eliminating the quadratic term also resulted in a nonsignificant linear term. Thus, although there is no average grade trend in the feeling of control over the activity, the other experiential components of self-worth exhibit a swing during adolescence with a low around Grade 10. These findings indicate discontinuity of experiential self-worth except for the feeling of control, which exhibits continuity.

Both linear and quadratic grade terms for the two affect variables, feeling good and feeling happy, were significant, describing a concave-up trend with lows

Table 4. *Multilevel Models Used for Testing Linear and Quadratic Grade Trends of Self-Concept, Experiential Self-Worth, and Affect Variables: Estimated Average Population Coefficients and Variance Components*

							Dependent Variables								
	S-E		L-C		EXPY		EXPO		SUCC		CONT		GOOD		HAPP	
Predictors	M	SE	M	SE	M	SE	M	SE	M	SE	M	SE	M	SE	M	SE
Fixed Effects																
Constant	2.807*	.244	2.792*	.021	7.632*	.663	7.057*	.702	7.626*	.474	8.369*	.610	9.623*	.573	7.223*	.308
Grade (Linear)	.042	.054	.019*	.006	-.208	.137	-.280	.145	-.199*	.100	-.196	.128	-.388*	.119	-.336*	.065
Grade (Quadratic)	-.001	.003	—	—	.011*	.001	.016*	.008	.011*	.005	.008	.007	.015*	.006	.011*	.003
Random Effects																
Between-Subject																
Constant	.135*	.012	.109*	.011	38.500*	2.619	42.230*	2.871	13.340*	1.050	25.600*	1.868	27.340*	1.898	5.843*	.448
Grade (Linear)	—	—	—	—	.382*	.027	.426*	.030	.128*	.011	.261*	.019	.266*	.019	.055*	.005
Constant, Grade (Linear)	—	—	—	—	-3.677*	.264	-4.054*	.291	-1.233*	.106	-2.480*	.191	-2.566*	.195	-.543*	.045
Within-Subjects																
Constant	.141*	.008	.145*	.009	5.008*	.034	5.768*	.039	3.980*	.027	5.638*	.038	3.994*	.027	1.622*	.011

Note: — refers to effects that were not not included in the model and thus are assumed to be equal to zero. S-E = global self-esteem; L-C = locus of control (E–I); EXPY = living up to one's own expectations; EXPO = living up to the expectations of others; SUCC = feeling successful; CONT = feeling in control; GOOD = feeling good; HAPP = feeling happy.

*p < .05.

projected beyond adolescence. Thus, unlike experiential self-worth, affect appears to decrease across the whole span of adolescence. The decrease is faster in early adolescence and progressively slower afterward. The trajectory is not a swing, as adolescents' affect appears not to recover. These findings indicate discontinuity in daily affective experience.

Tests of Potential Modifiers of Grade Trends

Table 5 shows the estimated average population coefficients and variance components, with standard errors, of the final multilevel models used to test the possible modifications in the average grade trends of dispositional and experiential variables due to gender, family structure, and ethnicity.

The model of global self-esteem contains simple main class effects, implying parallel trends, and one set of interactions involving the Hispanics, implying nonparallel trends. The global referent group is White and Native American adolescent boys not from reconstituted families. The simple main class effects indicate that adolescent girls, adolescents from reconstituted families, and Asian Americans have consistently lower self-esteem across adolescence; African Americans have consistently higher self-esteem across adolescence. Figure 1 shows the predicted average grade trends relative to the interaction of ethnicity with grade. The developmental trajectories refer to boys not from reconstituted families. Hispanics appear to have a disadvantaged entry to adolescence relative to African Americans and Whites, but not to Asian Americans, and they exhibit a spectacular recovery in global self-esteem; by Grade 10 they surpass Whites and Native Americans.

The model of locus of control contains only main class effects. The global referent group is not Hispanic and not from reconstituted or single-parent families. The main class effects indicate that Hispanics and adolescents from single-parent and reconstituted families consistently have a more external locus of control across adolescence.

The model of living up to one's own expectations contains only main class effects. The global referent class is Whites, African Americans, and Native Americans not from single-parent families. The introduction of new predictors made both the linear and quadratic grade terms nonsignificant. The model implies that perceptions of meeting one's own standards are constant across adolescence, and are consistently lower for adolescents from single-parent families and Hispanics across adolescence.

The model of living up to the expectations of others contains four simple main class effects and one set of interactions involving adolescents from reconstituted families. The global referent group is Whites and Native Americans from traditional and other families. The simple main class effects indicate that Hispanics, African Americans, Asian Americans, and adolescents from single-parent families have consistently lower perceptions of meeting environmental demands across adolescence. Figure 2 shows the predicted average grade trends relative to the interaction of family structure with grade. The developmental trajectories refer to Whites and Native Americans. The trends for adolescents from traditional, other, and single-parent families conform to a swing with a minimum achieved at about Grade 9. Comparatively, adolescents from single-parent families score remarkably lower across adolescence. On the other hand, adolescents from reconstituted families enter adolescence as low as the adolescents from single-parent families and show a remarkable resilience that peaks at Grade 10.

The model of feeling successful contains one simple main class effect and two sets of interactions involving adolescents from single-parent families and Asian Americans. The global referent group is Whites, African Americans, and Native Americans not from single-parent families. The simple main class effect indicates that Hispanics feel consistently less successful across adolescence. Figure 3 shows the two sets of predicted average grade trends relative to the interactions of family structure and ethnicity with grade. In the graph describing the effects of family structure, the developmental trajectories refer to Whites, African Americans, and Native Americans. Adolescents from single-parent families have a disadvantaged entry to adolescence but they recover almost entirely by Grade 10. In the graph describing the effects of ethnicity, the developmental trajectories refer to adolescents not from single-parent families. Although it presents a boost at Grade 10, the trajectory for Asian Americans is remarkably lower.

The model of feeling in control contains one simple main class effect and three sets of interactions involving family structure and ethnicity. The global referent group is Whites, Hispanics, and Native Americans from traditional and other families. The simple main class effect indicates that African Americans feel consistently more in control of the activity. Figure 4 shows the two sets of predicted average grade trends relative to the interactions of family structure and ethnicity with grade. In the graph describing the family structure effects, the developmental trajectories refer to Whites, Hispanics, and Native Americans. Adolescents from traditional and other families exhibit a swing with a low at about Grade 10, followed by a marginal recovery. Adolescents from single-parent families have a disadvantaged entry to adolescence but recover almost entirely by

Table 5. *Final Multilevel Models of Self-Concept, Experiential Self-Worth, and Affect Variables Regressed on Grade, Gender, Family Structure, and Ethnicity: Average Population Coefficients and Variance Components*

							Dependent Variables									
	S-E		L-C		EXPY		EXPO		SUCC		CONT		GOOD		HAPP	
Predictors	M	SE	M	SE	M	SE	M	SE	M	SE	M	SE	M	SE	M	SE
Fixed Effects[a]																
Constant	3.143	.259	2.860	.062	6.917	.067	8.154	.756	8.810	.537	9.454	.763	9.536	.609	7.154	.308
Grade (Linear)	-.016	.057	.019	.006	—	—	-.440	.156	-.403	.113	-.447	.159	-.325	.122	-.336	.045
Grade (Quadratic)	.002	.003	—	—	—	—	.024	.008	.021	.006	.021	.008	.012	.007	.011	.003
Gender																
Gender	-.138	.030	—	—	—	—	—	—	—	—	—	—	-.201	.104	—	—
Gender × Grade (Linear)	—	—	—	—	—	—	—	—	—	—	—	—	—	—	—	—
Gender × Grade (Quadratic)	—	—	—	—	—	—	—	—	—	—	—	—	—	—	—	—
Family																
Single	—	—	-.075	.037	-.289	.135	-.363	.165	-4.006	1.215	-5.593	1.598	—	—	—	—
Reconstituted	-.082	.042	-.114	.042	—	—	-5.050	1.998	—	—	-3.420	1.771	—	—	.165	.068
Other	—	—	—	—	—	—	—	—	—	—	—	—	—	—	—	—
Single × Grade (Linear)	—	—	—	—	—	—	—	—	.747	.259	1.145	.337	—	—	—	—
Reconstituted × Grade (Linear)	—	—	—	—	—	—	1.108	.415	—	—	.826	.371	—	—	—	—
Other × Grade (Linear)	—	—	—	—	—	—	—	—	—	—	—	—	—	—	—	—
Single × Grade (Quadratic)	—	—	—	—	—	—	—	—	-.035	.014	-.058	.018	—	—	—	—
Reconstituted × Grade (Quadratic)	—	—	—	—	—	—	-.059	.022	—	—	-.044	.020	—	—	—	—
Other × Grade (Quadratic)	—	—	—	—	—	—	—	—	—	—	—	—	—	—	—	—
Ethnicity																
Hispanic	-1.709	.724	-.143	.042	-.393	.145	-.866	.181	-.542	.112	—	—	—	—	—	—
African American	.183	.040	—	—	—	—	-.443	.170	—	—	.342	.129	.861	.134	.238	.061

(Continued)

135

Table 5. *(Continued)*

	Dependent Variables															
	S-E		L-C		EXPY		EXPO		SUCC		CONT		GOOD		HAPP	
Predictors	M	SE	M	SE	M	SE	M	SE	M	SE	M	SE	M	SE	M	SE
Asian American	-.161	.061	—	—	-1.150	.219	-.937	.263	-4.725	2.035	6.872	2.595	4.572	2.420	—	—
Native American	—	—	—	—	—	—	—	—	—	—	—	—	—	—	—	—
Hispanic × Grade (Linear)	.368	.163	—	—	—	—	—	—	—	—	—	—	—	—	—	—
African American × Grade (Linear)	—	—	—	—	—	—	—	—	—	—	—	—	—	—	—	—
Asian American × Grade (Linear)	—	—	—	—	—	—	—	—	.875	.420	-1.435	.531	-1.175	.489	—	—
Native American × Grade (Linear)	—	—	—	—	—	—	—	—	—	—	—	—	—	—	—	—
Hispanic × Grade (Quadratic)	-.019	.009	—	—	—	—	—	—	—	—	—	—	—	—	—	—
African American × Grade (Quadratic)	—	—	—	—	—	—	—	—	—	—	—	—	—	—	—	—
Asian American × Grade (Quadratic)	—	—	—	—	—	—	—	—	-.045	.022	.069	.044	.061	.025	—	—
Native American × Grade (Quadratic)	—	—	—	—	—	—	—	—	—	—	—	—	—	—	—	—
Random Effects																
Between-Subject																
Constant	.127	.011	.109	.011	3.183	.142	41.500	2.836	13.070	1.028	25.510	1.845	27.240	1.888	5.846	.446
Grade (Linear)	—	—	—	—	—	—	.418	.030	.128	.011	.260	.020	.264	.019	.055	.005
Constant, Grade (linear)	—	—	—	—	—	—	-3.986	.287	-1.224	.104	-2.477	.188	-2.562	.189	-.545	.045
Within-Subjects																
Constant	.138	.008	.145	.009	5.439	.037	5.768	.039	3.979	.027	5.635	.038	3.994	.027	1.622	.011

Note: — refers to effects that were excluded from the model and thus are assumed to be equal to zero. S-E = global self-esteem; L-C = locus of control (I–E); EXPY = living up to one's own expectations; EXPO = living up to the expectations of others; SUCC = feeling successful; CONT = feeling in control; GOOD = feeling good; HAPP = feeling happy.

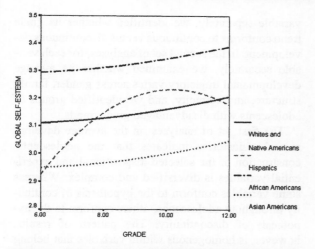

Figure 1. Global self-esteem: predicted average grade trends for adolescents from different ethnic groups. The developmental trajectories refer to adolescent boys not from reconstituted families.

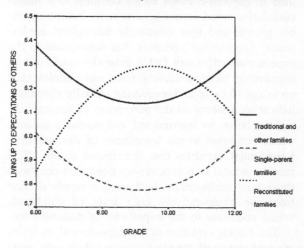

Figure 2. Living up to the expectations of others: predicted average grade trends for adolescents from different family structures. The developmental trajectories refer to Whites and Native Americans.

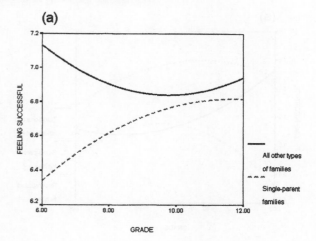

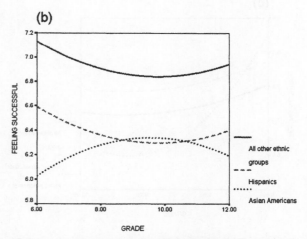

Figure 3. Feeling successful: predicted average grade trends for adolescents from (a) different family structures and (b) different ethnic groups. The developmental trajectories refer to Whites, African Americans, and Native Americans in (a) and adolescents not from single-parent families in (b).

Grade 10. Adolescents from reconstituted families enter adolescence at the same level as those from traditional families, keep growing up to about Grade 9, and then converge again with the adolescents from traditional families by the end of adolescence. In the graph describing ethnic effects, the developmental trajectories refer to adolescents from traditional or other families. For all ethnic groups the trajectory is concave-up, with a low at Grade 10, followed by a marginal recovery. Asian Americans enter adolescence with an advantage, decline sharply, and score remarkably lower by Grade 10.

The model of feeling good contains two simple main class effects and one set of interactions involving the Asian Americans. The global referent group is White and Native American adolescent boys. The simple main class effects indicate that adolescent girls feel consistently less good about themselves across adolescence, whereas African Americans

score consistently higher. Figure 5 shows the predicted average grade trends relative to the interaction of ethnicity with grade. Developmental trajectories refer to adolescent boys. Asian Americans score significantly lower and have a more pronounced swing, bottoming at about Grade 10, followed by a marginal recovery.

The model of feeling happy contains only two simple main class effects. The global referent group is adolescents not from reconstituted families and not African Americans. The simple main class effects indicate that adolescents from reconstituted families and African Americans feel consistently happier across adolescence.

Discussion

In this study, we conducted two sets of analyses. In the first set of analyses, we estimated the average de-

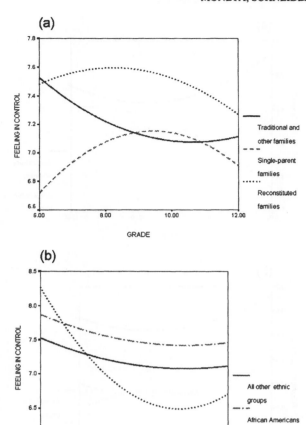

Figure 4. Feeling in control: predicted average grade trends for adolescents from (a) different family structures and (b) different ethnic groups. The developmental trajectories refer to Whites, Hispanics, and Native Americans in (a) and adolescents from traditional or other families in (b).

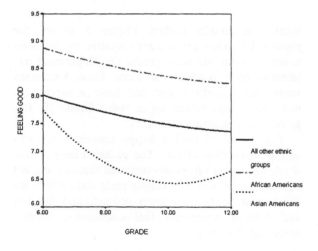

Figure 5. Feeling good: predicted average grade trends for adolescents from different ethnic groups. Developmental trajectories refer to adolescent boys.

velopmental trajectory of self-concept, experiential self-worth, and affect across adolescence, and, for each

variable separately, we identified whether its grade trend conforms to continuous versus discontinuous development. In the second set of analyses, for each variable separately, we examined whether its average developmental trajectory varies across gender, family structure, and ethnicity, and we identified groups of adolescents with disadvantaged grade trends.

The first set of analyses on the average developmental trajectories indicates that the adolescents' construction of the selected dispositional and experiential variables is diversified and complex. Whereas some variables conform to the hypothesis of continuity throughout adolescence, others conform to the hypothesis of discontinuity. The pattern of results, however, is homogenous within variables that belong to the same factors. The dispositional measures of global self-esteem and locus of control that contributed to the self-concept factor conform to a linear, cumulative trend across adolescence, indicating stable growth and thus continuity throughout adolescence. Experiential variables that contributed to the experiential self-worth factor generally conform to a concave-up trend, declining from early adolescence up to age 15 or 16 and recovering partially afterward, indicating a swing in the perception of accomplishment relative to internalized and social standards, which conforms to the hypothesis of discontinuity. Experiential variables that contributed to the affect factor conform to a concave-up trend that decreases throughout adolescence, indicating a steady decline from the comparatively high level of childhood, which conforms to the hypothesis of discontinuity.

The findings relative to the dispositional variables are consistent with the classic ego psychologists' view of development as a progressive buildup of ego structures and resources. Findings relative to the experiential self-worth variables are relatively new, as previous studies of age trends in experience investigated other, only partially related experiential components. The findings relative to the experiential affect variables are consistent with the observation that depressed mood is highly prevalent and visible during adolescence (Rutter, 1986), but they are in partial disagreement with Larson and colleagues' (1996) finding that affect during familial interactions recovers after middle adolescence because our analysis indicates no recovery. The difference in findings may be due to the fact that in this investigation we did not focus on possible differences of developmental trajectories across distinct contexts of action. Thus, it is possible that, although the aggregate level of affect declines steadily, its trajectory in specific social contexts deviates from the overall trend.

The fact that self-concept, experiential self-worth, and affect follow quite different developmental trajectories has an important implication for assessments of adolescence. The determination of whether adolescence is more of a critical phase or more of a transformation phase heavily depends on which psychological phenomena we look at. If we focus on dispositional variables contributing to the self-concept, we infer that adolescents' development is, on average, continuous. If, instead, we focus on experiential measures of self-worth and affect in daily life, we infer that adolescents' development is on average discontinuous. Insofar as discontinuity supports the storm-and-stress view and continuity disconfirms it, we have a mixed pattern of findings: In terms of self-esteem and locus of control there is no evidence of storm and stress, but the overall behavior of the experiential variables indicates the existence of storm and stress. Yet, these conclusions only refer to the average trend. The multilevel models that we estimated pointed out individual differences that we did not have the space to discuss in this article. The presence of individual differences in grade trends implies that individuals may deviate from the average trend by exhibiting continuity for variables that are on average discontinuous, and vice versa. Thus, these findings are consistent with Arnett's (1999) modified storm-and-stress view.

The second set of analyses highlighted several group differences in developmental trajectories. The findings relative to the possible gender modification are ambiguous. Adolescent girls scored consistently lower in global self-esteem and feeling good across adolescence, yet their developmental trajectories in the other variables were no different from those of adolescent boys. Thus, the findings are consistent with evidence that adolescent girls have lower self-esteem (Kling et al., 1999), but only partially confirm that adolescent girls have more negative self- appraisal in general (Gove & Herb, 1974). The fact that girls' disadvantage was limited in scope suggests that gender differences in developmental trajectories are the result more of social than biological determinants.

On the whole, adolescents from single-parent and reconstituted families had disadvantaged developmental trajectories compared to those of adolescents from traditional families. However, the pattern was not uniform, and these adolescents showed signs of resilience. Adolescents from single-parent families scored consistently more external in locus of control and lower in living up to one's own expectations, to the expectations of others, and feeling in control. Yet, they did not differ in global self-esteem and affect. Furthermore, although their scores on feeling successful were markedly lower in early adolescence, this difference vanished by middle adolescence. Being a child in a single-parent home involves a complex mixture of potential stressors such as traumatic events prior to parents' separation, financial difficulties, and social discrimination. The findings suggest that, although the effect of these stressors is visible, it does not extend to all components of self-concept, experiential self-worth, and affect.

Compared to adolescents from traditional families, adolescents from reconstituted families scored consistently lower in self-concept, equal in experiential self-worth variables and feeling good, and higher in happiness. Thus, although these adolescents seem to pay a price in terms of personality development, their everyday self-worth and affect appear well adjusted. On the whole, this group of adolescents appear to fare better than adolescents from single-parent families. Possible explanations include greater distance in time from traumatic events associated with parents' separation, fewer financial difficulties, and less social discrimination.

On the whole, ethnicity appears to be an important modifier of developmental trajectories. Differences were detected for all ethnic groups but the Native Americans, who were too small a subsample to achieve statistical significance. Compared to Whites, African Americans scored consistently higher in global self-esteem, feeling in control, and affect, and consistently lower in living up to the expectations of others. There were no differences in locus of control, living up to one's own expectations, and feeling successful. These findings are consistent with previous cross-sectional studies showing that African Americans have self-esteem levels at least as high as those of Whites (Simmons, 1978; Taylor & Walsh, 1979). Furthermore, these findings confirm the concomitance of high self-esteem and low sense of personal efficacy in African Americans (Hughes & Demo, 1989) in the form of high global self-esteem and low perception of meeting social standards. Several explanations have been advanced for this apparent paradox, such as the Black militance effect and the primary role of appraisal by significant others (Simmons, 1980), or the hypothesis that institutional inequality affects personal efficacy and not judgments of self-worth (Hughes & Demo, 1989). Whatever the interpretation, this investigation extends the finding of the apparent paradox by indicating that it characterizes the entire developmental trajectory of African American adolescents.

Compared to Whites, Hispanics were consistently more external in locus of control and scored consistently lower in living up to one's own expectations, to the expectations of others, and feeling successful; there was no difference in the feeling of control and affect. Their global self-esteem was markedly lower in early adolescence and exhibited a complete resilience by middle adolescence. Gaa and Shores (1979) found that, compared to Whites, Hispanic college students are significantly more internal in locus of control when experiencing success in intellectual performance and significantly more external when facing social failure. The fact that in our analysis the Hispanics were more external in locus of control and lower in experiential self-worth suggests that the lives of these adolescents may be characterized by more salient social failures, less salient successful experiences in academic domains, or both.

Compared to Whites, the Asian Americans scored consistently lower in global self-esteem, living up to one's own expectations, to the expectations of others, feeling successful, and feeling good. Although they scored higher in early adolescence, their feeling of control over the activity decreased more rapidly and was markedly lower by middle adolescence. There were no differences in locus of control and feeling happy. These findings are difficult to evaluate because Asian Americans have not been studied systematically to date. Yet, cross-cultural studies involving mostly Chinese adolescents and young adults have identified a self-effacing tendency that is often interpreted as a strategy for promoting group cohesion and social harmony (Yik, Bond, & Paulhus, 1998). Self-effacement applies to several person perceptions, with the exception of agentic traits like assertiveness and openness to experience (Yik et al., 1998), and results in lower frequency of positive self-statements but not in higher frequency of negative self-statements (Ip & Bond, 1995). Assuming that the Asian Americans tend to follow the same self-effacing pattern as the Chinese, the low values of self-esteem, feeling good, and experiential self-worth measures may be at least in part due to self-effacement. By the same token, the absence of differences in locus of control, a trait that is intrinsically agentic, may be due to the absence of self-effacement. However, this interpretation is at odds with the finding that Asian Americans report significantly more positive experiences than Whites while studying (Asakawa & Csikszentmihalyi, 1998). Therefore, we cannot rule out the possibility that the overall lower levels of daily self-worth exhibited by the Asian Americans are indeed indicators of developmental difficulties. Yet, the implications of these cultural differences for psychological adjustment are not straightforward. In particular, as hypothesized by Ip and Bond (1995), Asian cultural systems offer greater social support, so that individuals may need lower levels of self-approbation to maintain mental health.

On the whole, the findings indicate that there are marked differences in the developmental trajectories of self-concept, experiential self-worth, and affect across ethnic groups and family structures. The findings also highlight that, although some groups have less positive developmental trajectories, their disadvantage is not uniform across different dispositional and experiential variables and is not in all cases permanent across adolescence. Therefore, the global pattern is far from being bleak, as all groups of disadvantaged adolescents exhibit resilience.

Three limitations of this investigation should be emphasized. First, our analysis of the experiential variables did not make any distinction between the different social contexts within which adolescents' experience develops. Consequently, we were unable to study the likely compensatory effects across social contexts. By comparing our results on daily affect with those of Larson and colleagues (1996), we suspect that the developmental trajectories may differ across social contexts. For example, whereas affect during familial interactions improves after the middle point of adolescence, affect may keep deteriorating in other contexts. Yet, our data allow the modeling of developmental trajectories within contexts. In a future investigation, we will focus on two different facets of resilience: adolescents' capacities to find new, more optimal contexts for action and to reinterpret and positively transform contexts for action that are no longer satisfactory.

Another limitation of this investigation concerns the focus on the issue of continuity and discontinuity—that is, modeling only average experiential trends. We have also provided evidence on the issue of stability and instability—that is, quantifying the extent to which the ranking of the individuals within the sample is constant over time. Yet, studies of daily experience have found that, compared to adults, adolescents have greater frequency of negative affect and higher frequency of extremely positive affect (Larson et al., 1980; Larson & Richards, 1994). This finding suggests that development involves increasing capacity to control and regulate negative emotions coupled with a reduced capacity to experience peaks of positive emotions. If this trade-off forms during adolescence, then the within-subjects variance of emotions should become narrower with age. Yet, having modeled only average trends, we could only study the end result of the underlying emotional trade-offs. This type of modeling is the most natural in the presence of bipolar scales. Yet, in a future investigation, we will disentangle positive and negative sides of the scales and construct separate models for positive and negative self-perceptions to see whether the identified grade trends are mostly due to an increase in the rate of negative self-perceptions or to a decrease in the rate of extremely positive self-perceptions.

Finally, the observed differences in developmental trajectories across family structures and ethnic groups originated from an exploratory analysis, as we could not find any general theory to draw specific predictions. Thus, the existence of the differences that we detected in this study has to be confirmed with different samples, perhaps using different statistical methods. If confirmed, however, these differences call for a comprehensive explanation. The task requires an investigation of the potential roles played by family, peers, and scholastic environments. Ideally, this line of research will lead us to identify the factors behind family structure and ethnicity, possibly to the point of explaining totally the effects of family structure and ethnicity in terms of more specific underlying determinants.

References

Arnett, J. J. (1995). Broad and narrow socialization: The family in the context of a cultural theory. *Journal of Marriage and the Family, 57,* 617–628.

Arnett, J. J. (1999). Adolescent storm and stress, reconsidered. *American Psychologist, 54,* 317–326.

Asakawa, K., & Csikszentmihalyi, M. (1998). The quality of experience of Asian American adolescents in activities related to future goals. *Journal of Youth and Adolescence, 27,* 141–163.

Block, J. (1971). *Life through time.* Berkeley, CA: Bancroft.

Block, J. (1993). Studying personality the long way. In D. C. Funder, R. D. Parke, C. Tomlinson-Keasey, & K. Widaman (Eds.), *Studying lives through time* (pp. 9–41). Washington, DC: American Psychological Association.

Block, J. H., & Block, J. (1980). The role of ego control and ego resiliency in the organization of behavior. In W. A. Collins (Ed.), *Development of cognition, affect, and social relations: The Minnesota symposium on child psychology* (pp. 39–101). Hillsdale, NJ: Lawrence Erlbaum Associates, Inc.

Bryk, A., & Raudenbush, S. W. (1992). *Hierarchical linear models: Applications and data analysis methods.* Newbury Park, CA: Sage.

Cook, T. D., & Campbell, D. T. (1979). *Quasi-experimentation.* New York: Rand McNally.

Coopersmith, S. (1967). *The antecedents of self-esteem.* San Francisco: Freeman.

Csikszentmihalyi, M., & Larson, R. (1984). *Being adolescent: Conflict and growth in the teenage years.* New York: Basic Books.

Csikszentmihalyi, M., & Larson, R. (1987). Validity and reliability of the experience-sampling method. *The Journal of Nervous and Mental Disease, 175,* 526–536.

Csikszentmihalyi, M., Larson, R., & Prescott, S. (1977). The ecology of adolescent activity and experience. *Journal of Youth and Adolescence, 6,* 281–294.

Csikszentmihalyi, M., & Schneider, B. (2000). *Becoming adult: How teenagers prepare for the world of work.* New York: Basic Books.

Davis, M. K., & Franzoi, S. L. (1991). Stability and change in adolescent self-consciousness and empathy. *Journal of Research in Personality, 25,* 70–87.

Deci, E. L., & Ryan, R. M. (1985a). The general causality orientations scale: Self-determination in personality. *Journal of Research in Personality, 19,* 109–134.

Deci, E. L., & Ryan, R. M. (1985b). *Intrinsic motivation and self-determination in human behavior.* New York: Plenum.

Erikson, E. (1968). *Identity: Youth and crisis.* New York: Norton.

Freud, A. (1946). *The ego and the mechanisms of defense.* New York: International Universities Press.

Freud, A. (1958). Adolescence. *Psychoanalytic Study of the Child, 15,* 255–278.

Freud, S. (1910). *Three contributions to the theory of sex.* New York: N.M.D.

Funder, D. C., & Block, J. (1989). The role of ego-control, ego-resiliency, and IQ in delay of gratification in adolescence. *Journal of Personality and Social Psychology, 57,* 1041–1050.

Gaa, J. P., & Shores, J. H. (1979). Domain specific locus of control among Black, Anglo, and Chicano undergraduates. *Journal of Social Psychology, 107,* 3–8.

Goldstein, H. (1987). *Multilevel models in educational and social research.* London: Griffin.

Goldstein, H. (1995). *Multilevel statistical models.* New York: Halsted.

Gove, W. R., & Herb, T. R. (1974). Stress and mental illness among the young: A comparison of the sexes. *Social Forces, 52,* 256–265.

Hall, G. S. (1904). *Adolescence: Its psychology and its relation to physiology, anthropology, sociology, sex, crime, religion, and education.* Englewood Cliffs, NJ: Prentice Hall.

Hughes, M., & Demo, D. H. (1989). Self-perceptions of Black Americans: Self-esteem and personal efficacy. *American Journal of Sociology, 95,* 132–159.

Ip, G. W. M., & Bond, M. H. (1995). Culture, values, and the spontaneous self-concept. *Asian Journal of Psychology, 1,* 29–35.

Kling, K. C., Hyde, J. S., Showers, C. J., & Buswell, B. N. (1999). Gender differences in self-esteem: A meta-analysis. *Psychological Bulletin, 125,* 470–500.

Larson, R. W., Csikszentmihalyi, M., & Graef, R. (1980). Mood variability and the psychosocial adjustment of adolescents. *Journal of Youth and Adolescence, 9,* 496–490.

Larson, R. W., & Lampman-Petraitis, C. (1989). Daily emotional states as reported by children and adolescents. *Child Development, 60,* 1250–1260.

Larson, R. W., & Richards, M. H. (1994). Family emotions: Do young adolescents and their parents experience the same states? *Journal of Research on Adolescence, 4,* 567–583.

Larson, R. W., Richards, M. H., Moneta, G. B., Holmbeck, G., & Duckett, E. (1996). Changes in adolescents' daily interactions with their families from ages 10 to 18: Disengagement versus transformation. *Developmental Psychology, 32,* 744–754.

Loevinger, J. (1976). *Ego development: Conceptions and theories.* San Francisco: Jossey-Bass.

Loevinger, J. (1985). Revision of the Sentence Completion Test for Ego Development. *Journal of Personality and Social Psychology, 48,* 420–427.

Loevinger, J. (1993). Measurement in personality: True or false. *Psychological Inquiry, 4,* 1–16.

Longford, N. T. (1993). *Random coefficient models.* Oxford, England: Oxford University Press.

Marcia, J. (1966). Development and validation of ego identity status. *Journal of Personality and Social Psychology, 3,* 551–558.

Marcia, J. (1980). Identity in adolescence. In J. Adelson (Ed.), *Handbook of adolescent psychology* (pp. 159–187). New York: Wiley.

McCall, R. B. (1977). Challenges to a science of developmental psychology. *Child Development, 48,* 333–344.

Miyazaki, Y., & Raudenbush, S. W. (1999). *A test for linkage of multiple cohorts from an accelerated longitudinal design.* Manuscript submitted for publication.

Moneta, G. B., & Csikszentmihalyi, M. (1996). The effect of perceived challenges and skills on the quality of subjective experience. *Journal of Personality, 64,* 275–310.

Moneta, G. B., & Csikszentmihalyi, M. (1999). Models of concentration in natural environments: A comparative approach based on streams of experiential data. *Social Behavior and Personality, 27,* 603–637.

Moneta, G. B., Leclerc, A., Chastang, J., Dang Tran, P., & Goldberg, M. (1996). Time-trend of sleep disorder in relation to night work: A study of sequential one-year prevalences within the GAZEL cohort. *Journal of Clinical Epidemiology, 49,* 1133–1141.

Moss, H. A., & Susman, E. J. (1980). Longitudinal study of personality development. In O. Brim, Jr., & J. Kagan (Eds.), *Constancy and change in human development* (pp. 530–595). Cambridge, MA: Harvard University Press.

Prosser, R., Rasbash, G., & Goldstein, H. (1991). *ML3 software for three-level analysis: Users' guide for V.2.* London: University of London, Institute of Education.

Raudenbush, S. W., & Chan, W.-S. (1993). Application of a hierarchical linear model to the study of adolescent deviance in an overlapping cohort design. *Journal of Consulting and Clinical Psychology, 61,* 941–951.

Rosenberg, M. (1979). *Conceiving the self.* New York: Basic Books.

Rotter, J. B. (1966). Generalized expectancies for internal versus external control of reinforcements. *Psychological Monographs, 80*(Whole No. 609).

Rutter, M. (1986). The developmental psychopathology of depression: Issues and perspectives. In C. E. Izard & P. B. Read (Eds.), *Depression in young people: Developmental and clinical perspectives* (pp. 3–30). New York: Guilford.

Rutter, M., Graham, P., Chadwick, O., & Yule, W. (1976). Adolescent turmoil: Fact or fiction? *Journal of Child Psychology and Psychiatry, 17*, 35–36.

Simmons, R. (1978). Blacks and high self-esteem: A puzzle. *Social Psychology, 41*, 54–57.

Steinberg, L. (1990). Autonomy, conflict, and harmony in the family relationship. In S. S. Feldman & C. G. Elliott (Eds.), *At the threshold: The developing adolescent* (pp. 255–276). Cambridge, MA: Harvard University Press.

Taylor, M., & Walsh, E. (1979). Explanations of Black self-esteem: Some empirical tests. *Social Psychology Quarterly, 42*, 242–253.

Wheeler, L., & Reis, H. T. (1991). Self-recording of everyday life events: Origins, types, and uses. *Journal of Personality, 59*, 339–354.

White, R. W. (1959). Motivation reconsidered: The concept of competence. *Psychological Review, 66*, 297–333.

White, R. W. (1960). Competence and the psychosexual stages of development. In M. R. Jones (Ed.), *Nebraska symposium on motivation* (Vol. 8, pp. 97–141). Lincoln: University of Nebraska Press.

White, R. W. (1963). Sense of interpersonal competence: Two case studies and some reflections on origins. In R. W. White (Ed.), *The study of lives* (pp. 72–93). New York: Prentice Hall.

Wylie, R. (1979). *The self-concept: Vol. 2. Theory and research on selected topics.* Lincoln: University of Nebraska Press.

Yik, M., Bond, M. H., & Paulhus, D. L. (1998). Do Chinese self-enhance or self-efface? It's a matter of domain. *Personality and Social Psychology Bulletin, 24*, 399–400.

Received December 17, 1999
Final revision received July 20, 2000
Accepted September 18, 2000

Applied Developmental Science
2001, Vol. 5, No. 3, 143–157

Facilitating Adolescents' Constructive Use of Time in One-Parent Families

Reed Larson, Jodi Dworkin, and Sally Gillman
University of Illinois, Urbana/Champaign

Many adolescents in 1-parent families experience positive conditions for development. In this article, we use experience sampling data from 101 mother-only families to evaluate factors associated with adolescents' devotion of time to constructive activities, such as reading, sports, creative, and religious activities. Findings show that a set of family management variables, including firm discipline, family routines, and mothers' amount of time spent in child-supportive activities, were associated with adolescents' constructive use of free time. Adolescents' constructive time was also correlated with mothers' time spent reading, participating in religious activities, and watching TV; and with mothers' well-being and cooperation with the nonresident father. These results demonstrate how many families adjust positively to the situation of single parenthood.

It is a well-kept secret that many young people growing up in one-parent families do quite well. From reading the popular press and much of the research literature, one is given the impression that living in a single-parent family has a uniformly detrimental effect and that single-parent families inevitably provide a less favorable environment for children's upbringing. Yet, the variability in well-being among adolescents in one-parent families is as great or greater than that among adolescents in ever-married households (Hetherington, 1993). Evidence suggests that the proportion of youth with problem behaviors is higher in one-parent families, but the majority of youngsters in these families are in the range of being adequately to well-adjusted (Acock & Demo, 1994; Hetherington, 1993). The creativity literature even suggests that there may be a greater frequency of highly creative individuals from these families (Amabile, 1996; Simonton, 1994). Clearly many families adapt well to a one-parent household structure and provide a positive environment that facilitates the development of children and adolescents.

For applied developmental science, it may be more important to gain knowledge of these well-functioning one-parent families and how they have

adapted than to get further information about those that have not. Knowledge of the conditions of successful development is essential for effective policy and practice (Masten & Coatsworth, 1998). Single parenthood imposes challenges to daily family functioning: In addition to the economic hardships that affect many, one-parent families have less net adult time to carry out household and parenting tasks. More depends on the single adult, on how well she or he can manage with limited resources of time and energy. Applied developmental science can benefit from understanding how successful families adapt to the exigencies of single parenthood and provide healthy daily experiences for youth.

In this article we focus on this provision of developmentally positive daily experiences. We ask what features of single-parent families are related to children's spending time in developmentally constructive activities. What characterizes families—particularly the parents of families—in which youth spend their discretionary time in contexts associated with positive development, rather than watching TV or hanging out? We address this question with mother-headed families because they account for the great majority of one-parent families in the United States and elsewhere (Burns & Scott, 1994; U.S. Census Bureau, 1998). We focus on families with adolescents because single parents often see this as a difficult age period (Richards & Schmiege, 1993). Our empirical analyses explore the role of family routines, single parents' own use of time, parents' mental health, parents' employment hours, and the quality of cooperation with a nonresident father as factors affecting adolescents' constructive use of time.

This research was supported by grants to Reed Larson from the William T. Grant Foundation (95110689) and the National Institute of Child Health and Human Development (1 R03 HD35082).

We are grateful to Marcelo Diversi, Kadee Kurlakowsky, Tricia Joyner, Traci Lanning, Suzanne Wilson, Gretchen Wood, David Zanton, and many others for assistance with the data collection and coding.

Requests for reprints should be sent to Reed Larson, Department of Human and Community Development, 1105 West Nevada Street, University of Illinois, Urbana, IL 61801. E-mail: larsonR@uiuc.edu

Adolescents' Constructive Use
of Free Time

The dependent variables for this study are adolescents' uses of time. Theory and research suggest that some uses of time facilitate development, whereas others have a neutral or even negative relation to development. Larson and Verma (1999) theorized that each context of time use "engages participants in a milieu of rules, scripts, and goals, and each is associated with differing emotional and motivational experiences. Each also engages participants' attention in a distinct life world of information" (p. 702). More time in a context, therefore, is associated with the probability of more exposure to and participation in the experiences associated with that context. Of course, not all youth participating in an activity will have the same developmental experience: Two youth in the same arts club or on the same sports team can experience dramatically differing microenvironments. Nonetheless, amount of time spent in a constructive activity can be viewed as a proxy variable for the probability of positive developmental experiences.

Indeed, research substantiates that certain uses of free time have a longitudinal relation with indicators of positive development. Adolescents' involvement in arts, music, and other creative activities has been found to be independently related to improved school performance, high school graduation, college attendance, and adult artistic participation (Bloom, 1985; Eccles & Barber, 1999; Larson, 2000; Scott & Willits, 1989). Involvement in sports has been found to be associated with positive physiological effects, improved mental health (Brown & Lawton, 1986; Brown & Siegel, 1988; Tkachuck & Martin, 1999), improved school performance, high school graduation, and college attendance (Eccles & Barber, 1999; Mahoney & Cairns, 1997; McNeal, 1995; Otto & Alwin, 1977), although also with great likelihood of alcohol use (Eccles & Barber, 1999). There have been fewer longitudinal studies on the developmental benefits of reading, but research suggests an association with adult creativity (Simonton, 1994). Finally, cross-sectional research with controls for possible confounding variables suggests an association between participation in religious activities and prosocial values, psychological well-being, and lower involvement in risk behaviors (Brega & Coleman, 1999; Donahue & Benson, 1995; Donelson, 1999). Based on this research, we selected these four categories as the constructive uses of time to be evaluated in this study.

By contrast, other uses of free time have nonconstructive or negative relations with development. An enormous body of research has shown that spending a large amount of time watching commercial entertainment TV (which accounts for nearly all of adolescents' viewing), in addition to taking time away from other activities, has a longitudinal relation with aggression, obesity, poorer school performance, and other undesirable developmental outcomes (Huston & Wright, 1998; Rubenstein, 1983; Strasburger, 1995). Longitudinal research also indicates that a large amount of time spent "hanging out" in unstructured activities away from home is related to deviant behaviors (Osgood, Wilson, O'Malley, Bachman, & Johnston, 1996). We consider these nonconstructive uses of time.

A handful of studies suggest that, on average, youth in one-parent families may spend less time in some of these constructive activities and more time in nonconstructive activities (specifically watching TV) than similar youth in two-parent families. Employing data from a national sample of 492 participants, Meeks and Mauldin (1990) found that children and adolescents in one-parent families reported half as much time in structured leisure activities, including participation in lessons, competitive sports, and organizations, than youth in two-parent families. Other analyses of the same data suggested that children and adolescents in one-parent families spent less time reading and they watched TV for an average of 1 hr more per day than those children in two-parent families (Timmer, Eccles, & O'Brien, 1985). Bianchi and Robinson (1997) failed to confirm the difference in TV viewing for a sample of 3- to 11-year-olds. However, with a sample of young adolescents, Asmussen and Larson (1991) confirmed that youth in one-parent, as compared to two-parent, families spent less time in active leisure, including sports, games, and creative activities.

These findings suggest that, in general, conditions in one-parent families may be somewhat less favorable to supporting adolescents' constructive uses of time. Research suggests that constructive leisure often requires more coordination of family timetables, transportation, use of spaces, and other resources than do other leisure activities (Meeks & Mauldin, 1990). This is possibly more difficult when there is only one parent in the household. In contrast, nonconstructive uses of time typically involve less planning, coordination, or input from parents. Watching TV, for example, is often a "default activity" that is done when no other options are available (Larson & Verma, 1999). Of course, the lower average family incomes of single-parent families might also be a factor: Participation in some constructive activities costs money, and TV watching may be more frequent in one-parent families because it is inexpensive (Timmer et al., 1985).

Rather than focusing on these differences between one- and two-parent families, we think it most helpful to investigate differences among one-parent families. Comparisons between one- and two-parent families are inevitably confounded by numerous variables that make them incomparable; what is more useful is to look at differences within one-parent families, all of which face the similar situation of running a household with only one adult (Hoffman & Nye, 1975; Spitze, 1988). Indeed these prior time-budget studies all found large variability in constructive and nonconstructive time within one-parent families. Much can be learned by understanding what happens in some of these families that permits or encourages adolescents' constructive time.

Negentropic Family Systems

We hypothesize that one-parent families differ substantially in the degree to which their daily functioning supports adolescents' participation in these constructive, as opposed to nonconstructive, activities. At an abstract level, we theorize that daily life in some families is more ordered or negentropic (Csikszentmihalyi & Larson, 1984); that is, there is structure, predictability, available energy, and other resources that provide conditions for adolescent development. These families are organized and have the resources, supports, and coordination for adolescents to engage in developmental activities. In contrast, the daily lives of other families are entropic: They lack order, predictability, and available energy to permit or encourage adolescents' involvement in constructive activities. Disorganization may even interfere and disrupt adolescents' participation. Negentropy and entropy are abstract, hypothetical constructs that are difficult to measure, but they provide a heuristic for thinking about what variables affect adolescents' use of time.

Parents, we think, are critical to the cultivation of negentropy in families (see also Csikszentmihalyi & Rathunde, 1998). In one-parent families, the actions and daily patterns of the single parent are likely to be particularly critical. For example, past research suggests that children's well-being is more affected by a parent's well-being in one-parent versus two-parent families (Amato, 1993; Simons & Associates, 1996). Thus, we focus mainly on exploring various parent variables.

Family Management as a Predictor of Adolescents' Constructive Uses of Time

A new theoretical perspective stresses the executive role that parents play as managers of children's daily worlds (Furstenberg, Cook, Eccles, Elder, & Sameroff, 1999). Effective parents help coordinate the different parts of adolescents' lives. They orchestrate, instruct, discipline, provide support, and supply other important physical and psychological resources to their children. This family management perspective elaborates how, in direct and sometimes unconscious ways, parents organize, facilitate, and regulate the set of experiences that make up adolescents' daily lives. In our words,

they create negentropy that serves adolescents' well-being and development. Substantiating this perspective, Furstenberg et al. (1999) found that the degree to which parents played a role in these management functions was an important predictor of adolescents' well-being. These researchers and others (Jarrett, 1997; Richards, 1989) have found that, even in conditions of poverty, many single parents adapt creative management strategies that provide healthy daily experiences for their children.

In this study we examine three variables that reflect family management. First, we consider mothers' amount of time devoted to child-supportive activities, such as organizing the family's schedule, buying art materials, and providing transportation for the adolescent. When single parents devote more time to these supportive activities, we expect that their children will be more able to participate in constructive activities. Second, we consider the presence of family routines, including having meals at regular times, knowing when mother will come home, and having a clear division of chores. We hypothesize that these routines make family life more predictable, facilitate communication and coordination with parents, and thus provide conditions where teens are able to or can be encouraged to engage in constructive uses of time. Prior research shows that many single parents provide a structured, routinized home environment, and the children of these parents have higher academic achievement and better mental health than other children in one-parent families (Brody & Flor, 1997; Florsheim, Tolan, & Gorman-Smith, 1998). Third, we consider firm parenting, which includes enforcing rules and maintaining parental control. Research shows that, although rates of permissive and neglectful parenting are higher in one-parent families, many single parents exercise firm parental control (Avenevoli, Sessa, & Steinberg, 1999; Florsheim et al., 1998). When parents have firm control, we expect they will have greater ability to support and encourage adolescents' constructive versus nonconstructive uses of time.

Aspects of Parents' Daily Lives That Might Predict Adolescents' Constructive Uses of Time

Because single parents occupy a central position in the well-being of the family, various features of their daily lives, use of time, and well-being may also be related to adolescents' constructive use of time. First, we consider mothers' hours of employment. Single mothers have often been described as being time-poor, because they often have to work at a job while carrying full responsibility for the care of their families (Douthitt, Zick, & McCullough, 1990; Richards & Schmiege, 1993). Parents who work longer hours may be less able to provide support and encouragement for children's constructive uses of time. Time poverty, however, may be more of an issue for parents with younger children. Adolescents go to school for much of the day and have less need for constant care even when they are not in school. Duckett and Richards (1995) did not find a relation between hours of single mothers' employment and amount of time spent with adolescent children. Therefore, we test the relation of mothers' employment hours to adolescents' constructive time, but without a clear hypothesis.

Second, we evaluate whether the amount of time that single mothers spend in constructive and nonconstructive discretionary activities is related to adolescents' time in the same activities. When mothers frequently engage in an activity—whether it be a creative activity or watching TV—we would expect more engagement in the activity by children, either because they do the activity together or through parental influence. The former was illustrated in a study of two-parent families in India in which parents' and adolescents' rates of TV viewing were highly correlated, largely because TV viewing was usually a shared family activity (Verma & Larson, 1999). The latter would be illustrated in circumstances in which parents' participation in an activity, such as reading, sports, or religion, provides a model to children or reflects values or dispositions of the parent (e.g., religiosity) that are associated with other parent behaviors that influence adolescents' time.

Third, we speculated that single-mothers' emotional well-being might be related to adolescents' constructive use of time. Research indicates that depression and anxiety occur at higher rates among single mothers than in mothers in two-parent families (Davies, Avison, & McAlpine, 1997; Demo & Acock, 1996; Hetherington, Cox, & Cox, 1982) and that this is related to less effective parenting (Amato, 1993; Simons & Associates, 1996). Yet, many single mothers are not depressed or distressed, and many genuinely enjoy their lives. Although a period of distress often follows divorce, after a 2- to 3-year period of adaptation, the majority are well-adjusted (Booth & Amato, 1991; Hetherington et al., 1982). Many experience a process of renewal and a sense of psychological vigor in the mastery of running a family on their own (McLanahan & Booth, 1989; Mednick, 1987). We would expect psychologically vigorous and healthy single mothers to be better able to support their adolescents' constructive uses of time.

Finally, when the child's father is in the picture, we would expect the quality of the coparenting alliance to affect the adolescent's use of time. Acrimony and disagreements may interfere with effective parenting and coordination of the child's participation in constructive activities (Amato, 1993; Webster-Stratton, 1989). Some ex-spouses, however, are able to maintain a strong coparenting coalition (Morrison, 1995), and we would expect this to be related to adolescents' constructive use of time.

This Study

In sum, we hypothesized that the family management and other parental variables already discussed would be positively related to adolescents' constructive use of time and negatively related to adolescents' nonconstructive use of time. This article examines these relations with data from a volunteer sample of 101 comparatively educated one-parent families in central Illinois. We also consider the moderating role of adolescents' age and gender, time of year, and family income on these relations. Because the study is cross-sectional, we can only test correlations, not causal paths; and the limited sample size and statistical power of the relations does not permit evaluation of mediation or other complex multivariate relations. Given that we are dealing with a comparatively uncharted topic, our goal is to explore a range of variables rather than to test a mature theoretical model.

Methods

Sample

Participants in the study were 101 adolescents and their mothers in single-parent households from central Illinois. The adolescents included 54 girls and 47 boys, 10 to 19 years old ($M = 14.3$ years). The mothers ranged in age from 29 to 57 years old ($M = 42.7$ years). In 81 families, single parenthood resulted from a divorce, occurring a median of 7.0 years earlier (range = .2–17.0 years). In 6 families the mothers were separated, in 11 they had never been married, and in 3 they were widowed. The sample was recruited through newspaper and radio ads, fliers, and organizations that deal with divorced families.

These families provide a broad representation of single-parent families from central Illinois. Seventeen of the families were African American or biracial, 2 were Native American, 2 were Hispanic, and the remaining 80 were White. Thirty-seven lived in rural areas or towns with less than 5,000 people; 25 lived in midsized towns with populations below 50,000; and the remaining 39 lived in small cities with populations above 50,000. All but 7 of the mothers were employed, working an average of 40.0 hr per week (range = 4–60 hr). The median annual income of the mothers was $25,000 (range = $3,900–$70,000). The mothers were quite educated: All but 10 had some college education, 63 had a college degree, and 18 had graduate training. However, 30 families had been on or had applied for government assistance. Thirty-eight of the children

146

were only children. The average number of children in the home was 1.9 (range = 1–5). Only 5 households included preschool children. In 8 families there was an additional adult living in the household (a grandmother in 4, a roommate or friend in 3, and a boyfriend in 1).

Procedures

To assess participants' daily time use, we employed the Experience Sampling Method (ESM; Csikszentmihalyi & Larson, 1987). Mothers and adolescents in the study carried alarm watches during their ordinary lives and filled out reports on their activities and experiences at random times when signaled by the watches. Participants were instructed to keep the watch with them at all times (unless they decided to sleep during the signaling hours) and to fill out a report immediately after receiving the signals. Signals were scheduled between 7:30 a.m. and 10:00 p.m. On weekend days, signals were scheduled at random intervals of 1.0 to 2.0 hr, and on weekdays, signals were scheduled at random intervals of 1.5 to 3.0 hr until 3:00 p.m. and 1.0 to 2.0 hours after 3:00 p.m. In the analyses, these differences in the frequency of signals by time of day have been adjusted with weighting so that all times have equal representation. Mothers and adolescents received signals at the same time to permit analysis of simultaneous experience.

Most families participated in the ESM for two 1-week periods, approximately 1 month apart. Twenty-seven families provided reports for only 1 week. These 27 families did not differ significantly on any of the independent or dependent variables considered later, with one exception. Adolescents in families participating for 2 weeks reported higher rates of TV watching, $t = 1.99$ ($p = .049$). Most families participated during the school year, with 31 participating during the summer. These 31 families did not differ from the other 70 families on any of the variables, again with the exception of adolescents' TV watching, with rates of viewing higher in the summer, $t = 2.54$ ($p = .013$).

Participants provided a close-to-complete sample of reports on their daily experience. Assessment of responses to each signal for 37 families indicated that mothers responded to an average of 93% of the signals they were eligible to receive and the adolescents responded to an average of 84% of the signals. Mothers provided an average of 37.8 ESM reports during the first week and 35.7 during the second week. Adolescents provided an average of 32.2 ESM reports during the first week and 30.5 reports during the second week. These figures exclude times when signals were missed because the person was sleeping or the rare occasions when the watch malfunctioned. From data collected at the end of the ESM reporting, we determined that missed reports occurred for multiple reasons, including forgetting the watch or ESM report booklet at home, failing to hear the alarm signal, and being predisposed as when taking a test at school. These missed reports occurred during a wide range of activities and hence did not create a major bias in the estimation of time use (see Larson, 1989).

Mothers and adolescents in the study also completed a set of questionnaires and took part in semistructured interviews before and after the two ESM periods. For each week of participation, each participant received $20 and the family received $15.

Measures

Dependent Variables: Adolescents' Constructive and Nonconstructive Time

At each self-report, adolescents responded to an open-ended question asking, "What were you doing?" Responses were coded into 20 mutually exclusive activity categories, such as eating, transportation, resting, and watching TV (Larson & Richards, 1989). Adolescents' use of time was assessed by the percentage of ESM reports that each reported engagement in different categories of time use. For adolescents participating during the school year, ESM reports during school hours (prior to 3:00 p.m.) on weekdays were excluded from the computation of these percentages because this was not discretionary time.

Constructive use of time was represented by the percentages of time each youth reported being in four categories of activity: creative activities, sports, reading, and religious activities. We examine percentages for each activity, as well as a percentage for total time in all four activities. The category of creative activities was composed primarily of times adolescents were writing, playing music, doing art, and engaging in hobbies, such as sewing or building something. Sports included participation in team sports and individual sports, as well as a small number of occasions when adolescents were involved in other physically strenuous activities like dance or calisthenics. Reading included nonschool reading of books, magazines, and newspapers. Religious activities included attending church and participating in religious instruction.

We also computed the percentage of time that each adolescent reported in two categories of nonconstructive time. Time watching TV was the percentage of ESM reports during nonschool hours that the youth reported his or her activity to be watching TV. Given that nearly all adolescent TV viewing is entertainment TV, as opposed to educational TV (Larson, Kubey, & Colletti, 1989), we have not differentiated TV viewing by content. Time hanging out was the percentage of nonschool ESM reports that a youth reported being away from home; not with a parent; and not engaged in schoolwork, a job, or a constructive activity. The majority of this time (60%) was spent with friends; the most common activities were talking, idling, eating, and other leisure activities.

The percentages of time that adolescents reported different constructive and nonconstructive activities were employed as the dependent variables for the following analyses. In addition, we computed a score for total time in constructive activities, which was the sum of time in all four constructive activities. Because the raw percentages for all of these time variables were skewed toward 0.0%, we employed a square root transformation to make them more normally distributed, and these are used for all significance tests.

It should be noted that adolescents participating during the summer had more free time, but it did not result in higher percentages of constructive time. As reported earlier, for students taking part during the school year (but not the summer), we excluded ESM data points from the hours before 3:00 p.m. on weekdays. As a result the summer youth had more total ESM reports and more reports in the various activity categories. However, their percentages of this nonschool time spent in constructive activities did not differ significantly from those for the youth evaluated during the school year. They did not differ in total percentage of constructive time or in percentages of time within specific constructive and nonconstructive time categories, except TV viewing.

These different categories of time were relatively independent of each other. Reading was positively correlated with creative activities, $r = .20$ ($p = .045$), and negatively correlated with sports participation, $r = -.26$ ($p = .008$), but no other correlations between categories of constructive time were significant. Total amount of constructive time had a significant inverse correlation with TV viewing, $r = -.24$ ($p = .015$). Amount of time spent hanging out was not significantly correlated to TV viewing or any category of constructive time.

Independent Variables

We investigated five groups of independent variables.

Family management. We used each mother's ESM data to determine the percentage of her time that she devoted to child-supportive activities, like driving the child to lessons, helping with homework, attending a child's sporting event, and doing an activity with the child. Because these percentages

were skewed, we used a square root transformation to normalize their distribution. The scale of Family Routines was an instrument on the adolescent questionnaire used by Maccoby and Mnookin (1992) (possible range = 0–45; $\alpha = .81$). The nine items asked the adolescent to rate how predictable life was in the mother's home (e.g., I know when to expect members of the family to be home in the evening, I study in the same place each day, Chores get done when they are supposed to get done). We employed a shortened 12-item scale of firmness (vs. laxity) of parental control from the Children's Reports of Parental Behavior Inventory (possible range = 0–24; Burger & Armentrout, 1971; Margolies & Weintraub, 1977). Both adolescents ($\alpha = .80$) and mothers ($\alpha = .71$) completed the scale, and as their scores were only modestly correlated, $r = .30$ ($p = .003$), we use them separately.

Mothers' use of time. Employing mothers' ESM data, we computed each mother's percentages of time spent in all the categories of constructive time use for the adolescents. We also computed mothers' rates of TV viewing. We did not feel that the hanging out category was relevant for mothers and did not compute it. Unlike with the adolescents, there was not a rationale for excluding school (or work) hours from these calculations. As with other percentages computed from the ESM data, the distributions for these variables were skewed, so we used a square root transformation to normalize the distributions.

Mothers' emotional well-being. Mothers' daily enjoyment was computed from their reported emotion at each ESM signal. They rated their state on four items (happy, enjoying myself, cheerful, friendly) on a 4-point scale ranging from 0 (*not at all*) to 3 (*very much*). Values for the scale ranged from 0 to 12. The score used here was the average of each mother's ratings across all her ESM reports. Mothers' trait anxiety was assessed using Spielberger's (1993) 20-item Trait-Anxiety scale (possible range = 0–60; $\alpha = .90$). Mothers responded to the Center for Epidemiologic Studies Depression Scale measure of depression developed by Radloff (1977; possible range = 0–60; $\alpha = .88$). Prior research shows the scale to be strongly associated with clinical diagnosis of depression (Garrison, Addy, Jackson, McKeown, & Waller, 1991; Radloff, 1977). The Michigan Alcoholism Screening Test developed by Selzer (1971) was used to assess mothers' problem drinking. This 25-item self-assessment measure was used to determine alcoholism by assessing alcohol consumption and behavior (Skinner, 1979; possible range = 0–25; $\alpha = .98$).

Mothers' employment. Mothers' work hours were determined by a question on the questionnaire asking, "About how many hours per week do you work?" Mothers' time doing their job was determined by computing the percentage of ESM reports for which each mother reported her activity to be working at her job. Because the distribution of these values was not skewed, they were not transformed. Work hours and percentage of time working were correlated but not greatly, $r = .41$ ($p < .001$).

Cooperation between mother and father. Five measures of parental cooperation and coparenting taken from Maccoby and Mnookin (1992) were used, each based on an answer to a single, fixed-response question. Three questions assessed mother's perception of her cooperation with the child's father. The first asked for a rating from 1 to 10 of how much the mother was satisfied with the current arrangements for the child in terms of the amount of time the child spends with each parent. The second question asked whether the quality of the relationship with the other parent was friendly, businesslike, or hostile on a rating scale from 1 to 3. The third question asked for a rating from 1 to 6 of how often the parents talked to each other about the child(ren). There were two questions that assessed adolescents' perception of cooperation between his or her parents. The first asked for a rating from 1 to 4 of how frequently the parents spoke to each other in the past year. The second obtained a rating from 1 to 5 of parents' level of agreement about how much time each parent got to spend with the child. All five of these variables were coded as missing when there was not contact with the father. All five have been transformed so that higher scores represent more favorable cooperation and coparenting. Mothers' satisfaction with the current arrangements was not correlated with the other variables. The other four variables were intercorrelated (rs = .17–.57).

Analyses

The primary analyses for this article used the family as the unit of analysis and tested correlations between mother and family variables and variables for adolescents' use of time. Because the data are cross-sectional, we could not test causality, only the presence of correlations that would be consistent with causality. In several instances we were led to speculate on mediational relations among the independent variables; however, the sample was not sufficiently large and the strength of relations was not strong enough in any instance to satisfy the conditions for mediation (Baron & Kenny, 1986).

Results

Descriptive Data

As expected, there were wide differences among adolescents in the amount of time spent in constructive and nonconstructive activities. Total amount of time in constructive activities ranged from 0% to 42% of adolescents' reports, with an average of 10.7%. Time watching TV ranged from 0% to 67%; the average was 19.1%, which is almost twice the total time spent in constructive activities. Means and standard deviations for all the independent and dependent variables employed in the analyses are given in Table 1.

As a preparatory step to the analyses, we tested whether these variables differed by adolescent's gender and age, by the education level and income of the mother, and by time since divorce. Only one variable, adolescents' time in sports, differed by adolescents' gender, with boys reporting more time than girls, $t = 2.37$ ($p = .020$). Several variables differed by the adolescent's age (Table 1). Older adolescents reported significantly less time in constructive activities, including less time in creative activities and sports. When the adolescents were older, mothers reported less time in child-supportive activities and more time working; the adolescents also perceived there to be fewer routines in the family. This latter set of differences suggests family adjustments one might expect as children move into late adolescence. Given these age differences for both our independent and dependent variables, we partialed out age in all the following analyses.

Few differences were found related to mothers' education and income. Higher education was related to mothers' lower scores for problem drinking, $r = -.28$ ($p = .005$), and to less TV watching by the adolescent, $r = -.22$ ($p = .031$), but not to other variables. Mothers' income was related only to hours of employment, $r = .44$ ($p < .001$). Although low income is often seen as a significant factor affecting the functioning of one-parent families and the children in them, it appears not to be a factor for this sample.

Because the research literature typically suggests that there is an adjustment process requiring about 2 to 3 years following divorce (Hetherington, 1999), we tested whether there were differences in the divorced families between those within this 3-year period ($n = 19$) and the others ($n = 62$). We found differences for only two variables. Children reported more talk between parents when the divorce was recent, $t = 2.38$ ($p = .020$), and less time in religious activities, $t = -2.04$ ($p = .045$). We also evaluated whether any of the dependent or independent variables differed for the eight households that included an extra adult and found that they did not.

In sum, very few of our dependent and independent variables were associated with mothers' education, income, and time since divorce. Therefore,

Table 1. *Means, Standard Deviations, and Age Differences for Independent and Dependent Variables*

	N	M	SD	Age of Adolescent 10–14: M	15–19: M
Dependent Variables[a]					
Adolescents' Constructive Time					
Total Time	101	10.7	8.8	14.0	7.3****
Creative Activities	101	2.1	3.0	2.6	1.5**
Sports	101	4.3	6.8	6.4	2.1****
Reading	101	3.5	5.6	3.9	3.1
Religious Activities	101	0.8	2.2	1.1	0.6
Adolescents Nonconstructive Time					
TV Viewing	101	19.1	13.3	20.5	17.5
Hanging Out	101	3.0	3.1	2.6	3.5
Independent Variables					
Family Management					
Mothers' Child Support Activities[a]	101	3.2	3.8	4.7	1.7****
Family Routines	94	23.4	10.4	26.4	20.3***
Firm Parental Control (Child)	96	10.3	4.6	10.0	10.5
Firm Parental Control (Mother)	99	8.6	3.3	9.2	7.9*
Mothers' Free Time Activities[a]					
Creative Activities	101	0.8	1.8	0.6	0.9
Sports	101	0.7	1.4	0.6	0.7
Reading	101	3.5	3.7	3.4	3.6
Religious Activities	101	0.8	1.7	0.9	0.7
TV Viewing	101	8.1	6.2	7.3	8.8
Mothers' Well-Being					
Daily Enjoyment	101	7.4	2.0	7.2	7.6
Anxiety	100	19.8	10.2	20.4	19.2
Depression	100	11.5	9.8	12.0	11.0
Problem Drinking	100	1.1	1.3	1.0	1.2
Mothers' Employment					
Hours Per Week	89	39.6	10.1	37.3	42.1**
Time Doing Job (ESM)	101	25.5	13.7	21.9	29.4***
Cooperation Between Mother and Father					
Satisfaction With Arrangements (Mother)	81	6.3	3.5	5.7	6.9
Quality of Relationship (Mother)	67	2.3	0.7	2.1	2.4
Frequency of Talk (Mother)	73	2.8	1.2	2.9	2.6
Frequency of Talk (Child)	84	2.3	0.9	2.3	2.2
Agreement on Timing (Child)	61	3.2	1.7	3.0	3.5

Note: ESM = Experience Sampling Method.
[a]The table displays means for the raw percentage of time in the given activity. Significance tests by age were performed on values for these variables that were subject to a square root transformation.
*$p < .10$. **$p < .05$. ***$p < .01$. ****$p < .001$.

there was not cause to employ them as control variables in the following analyses. Only adolescents' age was controlled.

Family Management

Our first expectation was that adolescents' constructive use of time would be related to aspects of mothers' family management. We predicted this time to be greater when mothers put in more time in child-supportive activities, when there were family routines, and when mothers were firm as opposed to lax. To test these hypotheses, we evaluated correlations between adolescents' time and measures of these family management variables (Table 2).

Findings provided partial support for these expectations. Mothers' rate of participation in supportive activities had a significant inverse relation to adolescents' time watching TV, but no relation to constructive activities. Family routines had a significant positive relation to adolescents' total time spent in constructive activities. Finally, we found that adolescents', but not mothers', reports on mothers' firmness predicted adolescents' time in constructive activities. Mothers' perceived firm control was significantly correlated with adolescents' total time in constructive activities, time reading, and time in religious activities. Although mothers' and adolescents' perceptions of mothers' firm control were correlated, $r = .30$ ($p = .003$), mothers' ratings did not predict adolescents' time. This is consistent with past research suggesting that adolescents' ratings are more sensitive to the actual parenting environment they are experiencing (Gonzales, Cauce, & Mason, 1996; Noller & Callan, 1986).

In sum, adolescents' perceptions of family routines and mothers' firmness had significant positive relations to adolescents' greater participation in constructive activities. To evaluate whether each had independent relations to constructive time, we conducted a regression in which adolescent's age, family routines, and mother's firmness were independent variables. In this regression, both routines (β = .217, p = .027) and mother's firmness (β = .254, p = .007) were significant, suggesting that they make an independent contribution to adolescents' time in constructive activities.

Mothers' Employment

We next examined whether adolescents' time use was related to mothers' employment, including mothers' number of working hours per week as reported on the questionnaire, and the percentage of time that mothers reported themselves to be working at their jobs during the study, based on the ESM.

Contrary to the time-poor hypothesis, these two measures of mothers' employment showed little relation to adolescents' constructive use of time (Table 3). Mothers' ESM reports of time working at their jobs had a significant relation to less adolescent time in creative activities, but there were no other significant relations between mothers' work and adolescents' time in constructive activities. Neither measure of mothers' employment was related to total time in constructive activities. Speculating that different patterns might emerge for mothers who worked 50 or 60 hr per week, we also tested quadratic relations between mothers' hours and adolescents' time, but these tests did not reveal significant relations.

In sum, the data fail to provide a basis for arguing that mothers' longer working hours affect adolescents' constructive use of time. In fact mothers' working hours had a significant relation with their children watching less TV. We also did not find that the strength of the relation between mothers' working hours and adolescents' constructive use of time differed between families participating during the summer and school year. In addition, we had expected that mothers' number of evening work hours might predict adolescents' use of time, but we did not find this relation, perhaps partly because there were few

Table 2. *Partial Correlations for Mothers' Family Management With Adolescents' Constructive Activities, With Adolescents' Age Controlled*

	Constructive Time					Nonconstructive Time	
	Total	Creative	Sports	Reading	Religion	TV	Hanging Out
Mothers' Child Support Activities	.18*	.13	.18*	−.03	.02	−.21**	−.07
Family Routines	.29***	.15	.17	.04	.00	−.13	−.06
Firm Parental Control (Child)	.33***	.19*	.03	.21**	.25**	.01	−.01
Firm Parental Control (Mother)	.15	.08	.06	.06	.04	−.06	.00

*p < .10. **p < .05. ***p < .01. ****p < .001.

Table 3. *Partial Correlations Between Mothers' and Adolescents' Participation in Constructive Activities, With Adolescents' Age Controlled*

	Constructive Time					Nonconstructive Time	
	Total	Creative	Sports	Reading	Religion	TV	Hanging Out
Mothers' Employment							
Hours Per Week	.17	−.06	.20*	−.07	.08	−.28***	.16
Time Doing Job (ESM)	−.07	−.23**	.08	−.18*	.08	−.01	.17*
Mothers' Free Time Activities							
Creative Activities	.04	−.07	.07	.01	−.09	−.03	−.05
Sports	.07	−.08	.13	.07	−.01	−.16	.09
Reading	.21**	.10	.09	.25**	−.15	−.01	.02
Religious Activities	.39****	.05	.13	.20**	.44****	−.22**	.02
TV Viewing	−.21**	.01	−.23**	.03	.02	.17*	−.10

Note: ESM = Experience Sampling Method.
*p < .10. **p < .05. ***p < .01. ****p < .001.

women who had jobs that took up many evening hours per week.

Mothers' Use of Time

The third question was whether adolescents' use of time was related to mothers' use of time. Might adolescents spend more time in constructive (or nonconstructive) activities because their mothers spend time in those activities? To evaluate this, we examined the correlations between adolescents' and mothers' amount of time in each activity, both measured by the ESM. The associations for the same activities can be seen in the diagonal in the lower part of Table 3.

To our surprise, mothers' participation in an activity significantly predicted adolescents' participation in that activity for only reading and religion (Table 3). The correlation for reading was not attributable to mothers and adolescents reading together. Reading was not frequently a shared activity: When mothers reported reading on the ESM forms, adolescents reported reading for only 8% of the time. Religious activities, in contrast, were often done together: Adolescents reported participation in religious activities for 46% of the ESM reports when their mothers reported religious activities. Mothers' amount of time in religious activities also had a positive relation to adolescents' time reading and a negative correlation to adolescents' time watching TV. These off-diagonal correlations suggest that mothers' time in religious activities may be associated with values and dispositions that influence other parts of adolescents' lives.

Mothers' time in three activities was correlated with adolescents' total constructive time. Mothers' rate of reading and religious activities were associated with adolescents spending more time in con-

structive activities, and mothers' rate of TV viewing was inversely related to adolescents' time in constructive activities. To determine whether these three categories of mothers' time had independent relations with adolescents' total time in constructive activities, we entered all three (along with adolescents' age) into a regression predicting constructive time. In this regression, mothers' reading ($\beta = .20$, $p = .018$) and religious activities ($\beta = .33$, $p < .001$) were significant predictors, and TV watching was a close-to-significant predictor ($\beta = -.145$, $p = .087$). These findings suggest that these three variables make relatively independent contributions to adolescents' constructive time.

Mothers' Emotional Well-Being

We expected that when single mothers enjoyed their daily lives and their daily actions were not hindered by anxiety, depression, or problem drinking, there would be indirect effects leading adolescents to spend more time in constructive activities.

Our findings provided only limited support for this hypothesis (Table 4). None of the four measures of mothers' emotional well-being had a significant relation to adolescents' total amount of constructive time. There were, however, relations between mothers' well-being and adolescents' time in specific activity categories. Adolescents' time in sports had a significant positive relation to mothers' daily enjoyment and a significant negative relation to mothers' anxiety. Adolescents' reading had a significant negative relation to mothers' drinking. Adolescents' TV viewing had a positive relation to mothers' anxiety and depression. Adolescents' hanging out was positively related to mothers' problem drinking. These scattered findings suggest that mothers' well-being may influence adolescents' use of time.

Table 4. *Partial Correlations for Indirect Family Variables With Adolescents' Constructive Activities, With Adolescents' Age Controlled*

	Constructive Time					Nonconstructive Time	
	Total	Creative	Sports	Reading	Religion	TV	Hanging Out
Mothers' Well-Being							
Daily Enjoyment	.12	−.11	.23**	−.07	.14	−.10	−.03
Anxiety	−.14	.07	−.27***	.05	−.15	.23**	−.13
Depression	−.12	−.07	−.09	−.03	−.19*	.25**	−.16
Drinking Problem	−.17*	.00	.03	−.29***	−.10	.08	.22**
Cooperation Between Mother and Father							
Satisfaction With Arrangements	.17	−.08	.29*	−.01	.00	−.20*	.02
Quality of Relationship (Mother)	−.09	−.08	.09	−.19	.07	.03	−.20
Frequency of Talk (Mother)	.02	−.23*	.34***	−.26**	−.03	−.10	.10
Frequency of Talk (Child)	.24**	−.02	.33***	−.06	−.11	.05	.12
Agreement on Timing (Child)	.16	−.21	.36***	−.06	−.23*	−.07	.13

*$p < .10$. **$p < .05$. ***$p < .01$.

We had speculated that these relations would reflect a mediating role of family management, that mothers' emotional well-being influences their emotional resources for family management. However, we found that none of these well-being variables was significantly related to the family management variables; hence, these data do not provide a basis for substantiating mediation.

Cooperation Between Mother and Father

Finally, we expected that the quality of the coparenting arrangements with the adolescent's father would be related to adolescents' constructive use of time.

The findings provided partial support for this prediction (Table 4). Only adolescents' ratings of the frequency of parental talk were significantly related to their total amount of constructive time. There were associations, however, for adolescents' time in sports: Significant positive relations were found between four of the five measures of coparenting and adolescents' time in sports. This suggests that parental cooperation may be most important for supporting adolescents' constructive activities away from home. Contrary to expectation, mothers' reports on the frequency of mother–father communication were significantly correlated with less adolescent time spent reading. In sum, the findings suggest that positive interparental cooperation may have some influence on adolescents' spending time in constructive ways, particularly in sports.

Age, Gender, and Other Within-Sample Differences in Correlates of Adolescents' Constructive Time

We anticipated that the correlates of adolescents' constructive time might differ by adolescents' gender and age. Therefore, we separately computed correlations between all the independent variables and adolescents' total constructive time for boys and girls and for younger and older adolescents. Differences in correlations by gender and age were then computed using an r to z test.

Very few differences were found. There were no significant differences by gender. Mothers' anxiety was found to have a markedly stronger relation to younger, $r = -.37$, than older adolescents', $r = .06$, constructive use of time, $z = -2.18$, $p = .029$. Family routines had a significantly stronger relation to constructive time for older, $r = .50$, than for younger, $r = .07$, adolescents, $z = 2.33$, $p = 2.33$.

In addition, we tested whether these relations differed during the summer and between families with lower and higher incomes. We speculated that family management might have more influence over the summer, when adolescents had more free time, but in fact the opposite was the case. Family routines predicted constructive time during the school year, $r = .51$, but not during the summer, $r = -.11$, $z = -2.99$, $p = .003$; and firm maternal control was also a stronger predictor during the school year, $r = .45$, than during the summer, $r = .03$, $z = -2.02$, $p = .043$. We also thought that family management might be more consequential in poorer families, but found no significant difference in these variables between families where mothers' income was below or above the median of $25,000 per year.

Discussion

The purpose of this research was to understand well-functioning one-parent families. This is a group that is rarely studied or discussed, yet it can provide important information about positive adaptation to the exigencies of single-parent family life. Specifically, we were interested in identifying the features of one-parent families that are associated with adolescents spending their time in constructive versus nonconstructive activities. What happens in some one-parent families that permits and supports adolescents' engagement in activities related with positive development? The single mothers in the study faced a variety of challenges and demands associated with being a single parent, yet many were able to be good parents. Many of the mothers were able to cultivate an ordered family life that facilitated adolescents' experiences in contexts of positive development.

Family management variables emerged as features that differentiated well-functioning families. Two family management variables had significant and independent relations to adolescents' constructive use of time: firm parental control and family routines. Adolescents' perception that their mother exercised firm control was related to adolescents' total constructive use of time, time spent reading, and time spent in religious activities. Prior research suggests that single mothers, on average, are more lax than mothers in two-parent families (Avenevoli et al., 1999). An extreme example from the study was a mother who responded to a cutting comment from her daughter by getting in the car and going on a shopping spree, leaving her daughter and son alone at home to fend for themselves. Adolescents in our study had the most constructive time when their mothers were perceived by the adolescents as the opposite of this extreme example. These mothers maintained parental control and did not leave children to their own, or back off on expectations. In the interviews, many of these mothers described being actively involved in structuring and monitoring their adolescents' daily activities.

Family routines involved the perception that the family was an orderly system where daily activities were predictable and done on schedule. What may differentiate this variable from firm parental control is that it is less parent centered; the presence of family routines suggests distributed responsibility. The stronger salience of this variable for older adolescents may reflect a higher developmental stage in parent–child relationships where responsibility for creating and maintaining family order is shared. For older adolescents, who are more likely to be coming and going on their own, these family routines, this predictability, may facilitate their ability to expend their time in constructive ways. Being able to predict the behavior of their mothers and other family members allows them to be autonomous.

In a separate analysis of these data, we found that the evening schedule in these one-parent families was flexible and ad hoc, rarely fitting the pattern of "supper at 6:00 p.m." that we have found for similar U.S. two-parent families (Larson, in press). In examining individual cases it appeared that the mothers of adolescents with more constructive time managed their days so that this flexibility served the needs of the adolescent. For example, despite working 60 hr per week, the mother of the adolescent reporting the most constructive time arrived home at 4:00 p.m. each evening to prepare supper; check in with her daughter; and drive her to gymnastics, dance lessons, and religious instructions on various nights.

Our third family management variable, mothers' time spent in child-supportive activities, had a less clear relation to adolescents' use of time. When mothers spent more time in these activities, adolescents spent less time watching TV, but they did not spend significantly more time in constructive activities. The weak showing for mothers' supportive time may result because our categorization missed important management activities. Our measure did not include many mothers' supportive activities that took the form of talking with adolescents, the checking in and planning. Participants rarely gave us sufficient information on the ESM form to distinguish times when talk between parent and adolescent involved coordination and management. Our measure also did not include some of the intangible mental work of mothers (DeVault, 1991). Despite these limitations, our failure to find a relation between mothers' supportive time and adolescents' constructive time is important in suggesting that having large amounts of available time is not critical for successful parenting of adolescents by single mothers.

Indeed adolescents whose mothers worked more hours at a job were not handicapped in their amount of constructive time. As we suggested earlier, the image of single mothers being time-poor and unable to do what they need for their children may not be relevant for mothers of adolescents, because adolescents are in school for much of the day and need less direct care than young children. We thought that mothers' employment might make more difference when they worked evening hours or in the summer, but our findings did not support these predictions either. In sum, having a job was not inconsistent with single mothers' effective management of the family.

How mothers spent their free time, however, was related to adolescents' uses of their free time. In families where mothers read more, adolescents also read more. Because they were not reading together, this may reflect modeling, transmission of habits or values, or some other process. When mothers reported more frequent religious activities, adolescents did, too. This relation was partly attributable to them doing the activity together, possibly because of shared values or because some mothers expected their children to attend church with them. When mothers spent more time watching TV, adolescents spent less time in constructive activities. This suggests that mothers' TV viewing may take time away from supporting their children's constructive activities.

The other parental variables that we thought would affect family management and adolescents' constructive time showed only modest and inconsistent relations. Among the variables dealing with mothers' emotional well-being, we found that mothers' degree of problem drinking was related to adolescents spending less time reading and more time hanging out away from home. We also found that mothers' anxiety was associated with less constructive time for younger adolescents. It is possible that these relations are partly related to paths of causation in which mothers' drinking or anxiety interferes with her management of the family (Furstenberg et al., 1999), but the relations were not strong enough to provide an adequate test of this mediation model. We also found a relation between the quality of mother–father coparenting and adolescents' constructive time, especially with time spent in sports.

To summarize, this study finds preliminary evidence that family variables, particularly family management variables, are related to the amount of time that adolescents in single-parent families spend in constructive activities. We see family management as creating a negentropic, ordered daily family environment that facilitates adolescents' devotion of time and energy to activities associated with positive development. The findings do not permit us to determine whether these relations are unique to one-parent families; findings could be identical in two-parent families. We also lack the data to evaluate whether the well-functioning families in this sample had more or less of this daily negentropy than well-functioning two-parent families. In the interviews, we were frequently impressed that these families were as healthy and well-functioning as any other family. It is also relevant that mothers and children in our divorced families often reported that daily activities went more smoothly after the divorce without the father, which has also been found by others (Morrison, 1995; Richards, 1989). In some two-parent families, dissension between parents may interfere with this type of negentropy.

Policymakers and practitioners need to be aware that the majority of single-parent families function well and some provide very favorable environments for their adolescent children. In many cases, these families are best served by being left alone and freed from the stereotype that adolescents are handicapped. Research by Barber (1990) shows that, when teachers maintain high expectations for youth in families going through divorce, the school performance of these children is not reduced. Likewise, we have seen here that youth in one-parent families can be very involved in constructive free-time activities. Single parenthood is not inevitably a handicap. For single-parent families that do not show this high level of functioning, much can be learned from those families that do. An important policy goal is to provide the conditions for mothers and the family system, as a whole, to maintain firm discipline and family routines (Furstenberg et al., 1999).

Readers should be alert to the limitations of these findings and the need for replication and further elaboration. The mothers in this sample were relatively well educated, most had adequate income, and most lived in comparatively benign rural or small-city neighborhoods. Most of the divorced families were through the difficult period immediately after the divorce. Findings may differ for families in higher risk situations. In addition, we caution that the findings of this study are only correlational and do not prove causality. Past research indicates that the behavior of adolescents can affect the behavior of single-parents (Simons, Whitbeck, Beaman, & Conger, 1994); it is possible that the relations we have found reflect this reverse causality or, more likely, mutual causality, or the influence of unmeasured third variables, including family history and genetic dispositions.

Finally, we emphasize the limits of adolescents' time as a developmental variable. Evidence suggests that, in general, time spent in these constructive activities is associated with positive development, but that is not the case with all individuals. For example, the developmental benefits of sports depend on the adolescent's goal orientation (Roberts, Treasure, & Kavussanu, 1997) and the quality of coaching (Smith & Smoll, 1997). What is read (or watched on TV) and how it is interpreted is certainly important to what an adolescent gains from it. Participation in religious services may be less consequential than an adolescent's underlying spiritual life (Donahue & Benson, 1995). Time spent is only a proxy variable. Adolescents are

active participants in their development and just measuring time, without the underlying processes, gets us only so far. This article provides beginning evidence that single mothers' family management practices are related to adolescents' constructive use of time, but we must keep in mind the diversity and complexity of family life.

References

Acock, A. C., & Demo, D. H. (1994). *Family diversity and well-being.* Thousand Oaks, CA: Sage.

Amabile, T. M. (1996). *Creativity in context.* Boulder, CO: Westview.

Amato, P. (1993). Children's adjustment to divorce: Theories, hypotheses, and empirical support. *Journal of Marriage and the Family, 55,* 23–38.

Asmussen, L., & Larson, R. (1991). The quality of family time among young adolescents in single-parent and married-parent families. *Journal of Marriage and the Family, 53,* 1021–1030.

Avenevoli, S., Sessa, F. M., & Steinberg, L. (1999). Family structure, parenting practices, and adolescent adjustment: An ecological examination. In E. M. Hetherington (Ed.), *Coping with divorce, single parenting, and remarriage* (pp. 65–90). Mahwah, NJ: Lawrence Erlbaum Associates, Inc.

Barber, B. L. (1990). *The impact of family structure on the development of adolescents' family and work related values, beliefs, and aspirations.* Unpublished doctoral dissertation, University of Michigan, Ann Arbor.

Baron, R. M., & Kenny, D. A. (1986). The moderator–mediator variable distinction in social psychological research: Conceptual, strategic, and statistical considerations. *Journal of Personality and Social Psychology, 51,* 1173–1182.

Bianchi, S. M., & Robinson, J. (1997). What did you do today? Children's use of time, family composition, and the acquisition of social capital. *Journal of Marriage and the Family, 59,* 332–344.

Bloom, B. S. (1985). *Developing talent in young people.* New York: Ballantine.

Booth, A., & Amato, P. (1991). Divorce and psychological stress. *Journal of Health and Social Behavior, 32,* 396–407.

Brega, A. G., & Coleman, L. M. (1999). Effects of religiosity and racial socialization of subjective stigmatization in African-American adolescents. *Journal of Adolescence, 22,* 223–242.

Brody, G. H., & Flor, D. L. (1997). Maternal psychological functioning, family processes, and child adjustment in rural, single-parent African American families. *Developmental Psychology, 33,* 1000–1011.

Brown, J. D., & Lawton, M. (1986). Stress and well-being in adolescence: The moderating role of physical exercise. *Journal of Human Stress, 12,* 125–131.

Brown, J. D., & Siegel, J. M. (1988). Exercise as a buffer of life stress: A prospective study of adolescent health. *Health Psychology, 7,* 341–353.

Burger, G. K., & Armentrout, J. A. (1971). A factor analysis of fifth and sixth graders' reports of parental child-rearing behavior. *Developmental Psychology, 4,* 483–496.

Burns, A., & Scott, C. (1994). *Mother-headed families and why they have increased.* Hillsdale, NJ: Lawrence Erlbaum Associates, Inc.

Csikszentmihalyi, M., & Larson, R. (1984). *Being adolescent.* New York: Basic Books.

Csikszentmihalyi, M., & Larson, R. (1987). Validity and reliability of the experience-sampling method. *The Journal of Nervous and Mental Disease, 175,* 526–536.

Csikszentmihalyi, M., & Rathunde, K. (1998). The development of the person: An experiential perspective on the ontogenesis of psychological complexity. In W. Damon & R. Lerner (Eds.), *Handbook of child psychology* (5th ed., pp. 635–684). New York: Wiley.

Davies, L., Avison, W. R., & McAlpine, D. D. (1997). Significant life experiences and depression among single and married mothers. *Journal of Marriage and the Family, 59,* 294–308.

Demo, D. H., & Acock, A. C. (1996). Singlehood, marriage, and remarriage: The effects of family structure and family relationships on mothers' well-being. *Journal of Family Issues, 17,* 388–407.

DeVault, M. L. (1991). *Feeding the family: The social organization of caring as gendered work.* Chicago: University of Chicago Press.

Donahue, M. J., & Benson, P. L. (1995). Religion and the well-being of adolescents. *Journal of Social Issues, 51,* 145–160.

Donelson, E. (1999). Psychology of religion and adolescents in the United States: Past to present. *Journal of Adolescence, 22,* 187–204.

Douthitt, R. A., Zick, C. D., & McCullough, J. (1990). The role of economic and demographic factors in explaining time-use of single and married mothers. *Lifestyles: Family and Economic Issues, 11,* 23–51.

Duckett, E., & Richards, M. H. (1995). Maternal employment and the quality of daily experience for young adolescents of single mothers. *Journal of Family Psychology, 9,* 418–432.

Eccles, J. S., & Barber, B. L. (1999). Student council, volunteering, basketball, or marching band: What kind of extracurricular involvement matters? *Journal of Adolescent Research, 14,* 10–43.

Florsheim, P., Tolan, P., & Gorman-Smith, D. (1998). Family relationships, parenting practices, the availability of male family members, and the behavior of inner-city boys in single-mother and two-parent families. *Child Development, 69,* 1437–1447.

Furstenberg, F. F., Cook, T. D., Eccles, J., Elder, G. H., & Sameroff, A. (1999). *Managing to make it: Urban families and adolescent success.* Chicago: University of Chicago Press.

Garrison, C. Z., Addy, C. L., Jackson, K. L., McKeown, R. E., & Waller, J. L. (1991). The CES-D as a screen for depression and other psychiatric disorders in adolescents. *Journal of the American Academy of Child and Adolescent Psychiatry, 30,* 636–641.

Gonzales, N. A., Cauce, A. M., & Mason, C. A. (1996). Interobserver agreement in the assessment of parental behavior and parent–adolescent conflict: African-American mothers, daughters, and independent observers. *Child Development, 67,* 1483–1498.

Hetherington, M. E. (1993). An overview of the Virginia longitudinal study of divorce remarriage with a focus on early adolescence. *Journal of Family Psychology, 7,* 39–57.

Hetherington, M. E. (1999). Should we stay together for the sake of the children? In M. E. Hetherington (Ed.), *Coping with divorce, single parenting, and remarriage* (pp. 93–116). Mahwah, NJ: Lawrence Erlbaum Associates, Inc.

Hetherington, M. E., Cox, E. M., & Cox, R. (1982). Effects of divorce on parents and children. In M. Lamb (Ed.), *Non-traditional families* (pp. 233–288). Hillsdale, NJ: Lawrence Erlbaum Associates, Inc.

Hoffman, L., & Nye, F. (1975). *Working mothers.* San Francisco: Jossey-Bass.

Huston, A. C., & Wright, J. C. (1998). Mass media and children's development. In W. Damon, I. Sigel, & A. Renninger (Eds.), *Handbook of child psychology: Vol. 4. Child psychology in practice* (5th ed., pp. 999–1060). New York: Wiley.

Jarrett, R. L. (1997). African American family and parenting strategies in impoverished neighborhoods. *Qualitative Sociology, 20,* 275–288.

Larson, R. (1989). Beeping children and adolescents: A method for studying time use and daily experience. *Journal of Youth and Adolescence, 18,* 511–530.

Larson, R. (2000). Towards a psychology of positive youth development. *American Psychologist, 55,* 170–183.

Larson, R. (in press). Mothers' time in two-parent and one-parent families: The daily organization of work, time for oneself, and parenting of adolescents. In K. Daly (Ed.), *Minding the time in family experience: Emerging perspectives and issues.* Oxford, England: Elsevier Science.

Larson, R., Kubey, R., & Colletti, J. (1989). Changing channels: Early adolescent media choices and shifting investments in family and friends. *Journal of Youth and Adolescence, 18,* 583–600.

Larson, R., & Richards, M. (Eds.). (1989). The changing life space of early adolescence [Special Issue]. *Journal of Youth and Adolescence, 18*(6), 501–626.

Larson, R. W., & Verma, S. (1999). How children and adolescents spend time across the world: Work, play and developmental opportunities. *Psychological Bulletin, 125,* 701–736.

Maccoby, E. E., & Mnookin, R. H. (1992). *Dividing the child: Social and legal dilemmas of custody.* Cambridge, MA: Harvard University Press.

Mahoney, J. L., & Cairns, R. B. (1997). Do extracurricular activities protect against early school dropout? *Developmental Psychology, 33,* 241–253.

Margolies, P. J., & Weintraub, S. (1977). The revised 56-item CRPBI as a research instrument: Reliability and factor structure. *Journal of Clinical Psychology, 33,* 472–476.

Masten, A. S., & Coatsworth, J. D. (1998). The development of competence in favorable and unfavorable environments. *American Psychologist, 53,* 205–220.

McLanahan, S., & Booth, K. (1989). Mother-only families: Problems, prospects and politics. *Journal of Marriage and the Family, 51,* 557–580.

McNeal, R. B. (1995). Extracurricular activities and high school dropouts. *Sociology of Education, 68,* 62–81.

Mednick, M. T. (1987). Single mothers: A review and critique of current research. In S. Oskamp (Ed.), *Applied social psychology annual: Vol. 7. Family processes and problems: Social psychological aspects* (pp. 184–201). Newbury Park, CA: Sage.

Meeks, C. B., & Mauldin, T. (1990). Children's time in structured and unstructured leisure activities. *Lifestyles: Family and Economic Issues, 11,* 257–281.

Morrison, N. (1995). Successful single-parent families. *Journal of Divorce and Remarriage, 22,* 205–219.

Noller, P., & Callan, V. (1986). *The adolescent in the family.* New York: Routledge.

Osgood, D. W., Wilson, J. K., O'Malley, P. M., Bachman, J. G., & Johnston, L. D. (1996). Routine activities and individual deviant behavior. *American Sociological Review, 61,* 635–655.

Otto, L. B., & Alwin, D. F. (1977). Athletics, aspirations, and attainments. *Sociology of Education, 42,* 102–113.

Radloff, L. S. (1977). The CES-D scale: A self report depression scale for research in the general population. *Applied Psychology Measures, 1,* 385–401.

Richards, L. N. (1989). The precarious survival and hard-won satisfactions of White single-parent families. *Family Relations, 38,* 396–403.

Richards, L. N., & Schmiege, C. J. (1993). Problems and strengths of single-parent families: Implications for practice and policy. *Family Relations, 42,* 277–285.

Roberts, G. C., Treasure, D. C., & Kavussanu, M. (1997). Motivation in physical activity contexts: An achievement goal perspective. *Advances in Motivation and Achievement, 10,* 413–447.

Rubenstein, E. A. (1983). Television and behavior: Research conclusions of the 1982 NIMH Report and their policy implications. *American Psychologist, 38,* 820–825.

Scott, D., & Willits, F. K. (1989). Adolescent and adult leisure patterns: A 37-year follow up study. *Leisure Sciences, 11,* 323–335.

Selzer, M. L. (1971). The Michigan Alcoholic Screening Test: The quest for a new diagnostic instrument. *American Journal of Psychiatry, 127,* 1653–1658.

Simons, R. L., & Associates. (1996). *Understanding differences between divorced and intact families: Stress, interaction and child outcome.* Thousand Oaks, CA: Sage.

Simons, R. L., Whitbeck, L. B., Beaman, J., & Conger, R. D. (1994). The impact of mothers' parenting, involvement by nonresidential fathers, and parental conflict on the adjustment of adolescent children. *Journal of Marriage and the Family, 56,* 356–374.

Simonton, D. K. (1994). *Greatness: Who makes history and why.* New York: Guilford.

Skinner, H. A. (1979). A multivariate evaluation of the MAST. *Journal of Studies on Alcohol, 40,* 831–844.

Smith, R. E., & Smoll, F. L. (1997). Coaching the coaches: Youth sports as a scientific and applied behavioral setting. *Current Directions in Psychological Science, 6,* 16–21.

Spielberger, C. D. (1993). *Manual for the State–Trait Anxiety Inventory.* Palo Alto, CA: Consulting Psychologists Press.

Spitze, G. (1988). Women's employment and family relations: A review. *Journal of Marriage and the Family, 50,* 595–618.

Strasburger, V. C. (1995). *Adolescents and the media.* Thousand Oaks, CA: Sage.

Timmer, S., Eccles, J., & O'Brien, K. (1985). How children use time. In F. T. Juster & F. P. Stafford (Eds.), *Time, goods and well-being* (pp. 353–382). Ann Arbor: University of Michigan, Survey Research Center.

Tkachuck, G. A., & Martin, G. L. (1999). Exercise therapy for patients with psychiatric disorders: Research and clinical implications. *Professional Psychology: Research and Practice, 30,* 275–282.

U.S. Census Bureau. (1998). *Living arrangements of children under 18 years: March 1998. Unpublished Tables-Marital Status and Living Arrangements: March 1998 (Update)* [Online]. Retrieved July, 20, 2000 from the World Wide Web: http://www.census.gov/population/www/socdemo/ms.-la.html

Verma, S., & Larson, R. (1999). *Television in adolescents' lives: A member of the family.* Unpublished manuscript.

Webster-Stratton, C. (1989). The relationship of marital support, conflict, and divorce to parent perceptions, behaviors, and childhood conduct problems. *Journal of Marriage and the Family, 51,* 417–430.

Received January 12, 2000
Final revision received July 5, 2000
Accepted September 18, 2000

Applied Developmental Science
2001, Vol. 5, No. 3, 158–171

Family Context and the Development of Undivided Interest: A Longitudinal Study of Family Support and Challenge and Adolescents' Quality of Experience

Kevin Rathunde
University of Utah

Adolescents' perceptions of family support and challenge, and their quality of subjective experience and interest, were investigated over a 2-year period in a national sample of adolescents (Grades 6–12). In Years 1 and 3 of the study, 247 adolescents with diverse socioeconomic and ethnic backgrounds responded to the Experience Sampling Method and completed questionnaires that contained items on family support and challenge. The main findings show that adolescents who perceived more family support in Year 1 reported more positive moods 2 years later. Adolescents who perceived more family challenge in the base year reported a stronger focus on goals in Year 3. Perceptions of increased family support across the 2 years of the study were linked to positive changes in adolescents moods. Increases in family challenge combined with increases in support were associated with a stronger focus on goals perceived as important by adolescents. Increases in support and challenge were also linked with the development of undivided interest, or a synchrony of positive moods while engaging important goals. In contrast, adolescents from more permissive families (high support and low challenge) and from more authoritarian families (low support and high challenge) reported more divided interest (i.e., an asynchrony of moods and goals) 2 years later. These findings are discussed in terms of how family contexts may influence the development of undivided interest and adolescents' capacities for self-regulation and lifelong learning.

The quality of a family context can have a strong impact on adolescent development. Observational studies, for instance, have shown that a supportive and challenging family dialogue is more enjoyable for family members (Rathunde, 1997), and it is beneficial for adolescents' identity formation (Cooper, Grotevant, & Condon, 1983), ego development (Hauser, 1991), and moral and political reasoning (Boyes & Allen, 1993; Walker & Taylor, 1991). Other studies using a variety of methodological approaches have shown that parents who combine responsiveness with demandingness (i.e., an authoritative pattern) facilitate adolescents' academic achievement (Baumrind, 1989; Lamborn, Mounts, Steinberg, & Dornbusch, 1991; Steinberg, Lamborn, Dornbusch, & Darling, 1992), adjustment to divorce and remarriage (Avenevoli, Sessa, & Steinberg, 1999), self-regulation (Strage, 1998), and positive styles of coping (McIntyre & Dusek, 1995). Moreover, several studies suggest that adolescents from various ethnic backgrounds benefit from authoritative pa-

renting (see Mantzicopoulos & Oh-Hwang, 1998; Steinberg, Mounts, Lamborn, & Dornbusch, 1991; Taylor, Hinton, & Wilson, 1995).

A common theme investigated in many of these family studies is the balance between two important dimensions of family life that could be referred to as love and discipline. Each dimension is seen as important by itself, and each is important as a corrective for the other. Thus, when they are out of balance, a family risks being too permissive and inconsistent (love without discipline), or too rigid and authoritarian (discipline without love). Both of these extremes in the family have been linked to negative outcomes for adolescents, such as risky behaviors and substance abuse (Jackson, Henriksen, & Foshee, 1998).

Although these dynamics are well known and often discussed in the literature on adolescents, few researchers have attempted to articulate a link to similar family dynamics in infancy and early childhood development. The advantage of articulating this link, especially for this study, is that research on infants and young children has focused on the relation between family dynamics and states of optimal arousal in children. In other words, family environments have more often been thought about in terms of how they help reg-

Requests for reprints should be sent to Kevin Rathunde, Department of Family and Consumer Studies, University of Utah, 225 S. 1400 E. Rm. 228, Salt Lake City, UT 84112-0080. E-mail: kevin.rathunde@fcs.utah.edu

ulate children's arousal. Freud's (1933) perspective on parenting, for instance, suggested that with maturation, and the emergence of new erogenous zones that become the focus of a child's attention, parents needed to avoid overindulgence and overrestriction when interacting with the child. Healthy ego development depended on not being a slave to one's desires or to society's norms, and early parental involvement was seen as crucial in the long-term development of such a flexible ego. Elaborating on this tradition, attachment researchers have also called attention to the importance of optimal arousal for an infant's secure attachment. With sensitivity to momentary needs, parents must help lower a child's arousal through comfort, and sometimes raise it through stimulation. A parent's skill and timing in maintaining an infant's optimal arousal affects the emerging capacity for self-regulation (Field, 1985).

Rogoff's (1990) studies of early childhood approach the issue of optimal arousal from a Vygotskian perspective, but the themes are similar. Rogoff suggested that a parent's central job is to guide children's participation in activities in an optimally stimulating way, "through material arrangements of children's activities and responsibilities as well as through interpersonal communication, with children observing and participating at a comfortable but slightly challenging level" (p. 18). Thus, parents must learn when to support and when to challenge their children to keep them in the *zone of proximal development,* a zone of optimal arousal wherein the growth of mastery and self-efficacy are more likely to take place.

A full review of other relevant studies is not possible here, but the examples given serve to place this study of adolescents in a larger theoretical context of family contexts and children's optimal arousal (for a more in-depth review, see Csikszentmihalyi & Rathunde, 1998). This is an appropriate context in that this study emphasizes experiential outcomes and optimal states when an adolescent is more fully engaged with some task. Before articulating in more detail how the family is presumably related to such outcomes, it is necessary to say more about the importance of experience.

What Is Undivided Interest?

The experiential approach adopted here builds on insights from James (1890), Dewey (1913, 1938), and Csikszentmihalyi (1990). In a classic passage on the "varieties of attention," James (1890, pp. 416–424) distinguished a *passive* or immediate mode when interest was effortless, and an *active* or voluntary mode when an effort was made to focus attention and filter out irrelevant stimuli to maintain interest. James also laid a foundation for understanding how these two modes worked together for productive

ends. He recognized that the passive-immediate mode was typical of children and characterized by an "extreme mobility of attention." If such mobility did not come under increased control with maturity, however, it resulted in an unproductive pattern of mind-wandering in adulthood. More organized interests, therefore, included determined effort or voluntary attention that helped sustain interest and develop impressions that were, at first, vague or confusing. Furthermore, because voluntary attention could not be sustained for more than a few seconds at a time, the two modes had to work together to maintain interest. James commented:

> What is called sustained voluntary attention is a repetition of successive efforts which bring the topic to the mind. The topic once brought back, if a congenial one, *develops*; and if its development is interesting it engages the attention passively for a time. (p. 420)

Under favorable conditions, this dialectic proceeded for hours at a time as the object of attention went through continual development and change. Constant variation emerged from these passive–active shifts, and such variation was essential for holding interest. James identified the ability to sustain interest as a mark of genius and associated it with intellectual achievement (see also Rathunde, 1995). In contrast, this conversation of passive and active attention was often divided in a "common man," and interests, therefore, became disorganized.

Dewey (1913, 1938), in concert with James's insights, applied these dynamics of attention more fully to the domain of education. Like James, he believed that if immediate interest was separated from a long-term focus on desired goals, effective thinking would be blocked. He commented, "Experiences may be so disconnected from one another that, while each is agreeable or even exciting in itself, they are not linked cumulatively to one another" (Dewey, 1938, p. 26). Dewey (1933) described this dialectic in a variety of ways and sometimes used the terms *play* and *work* to evoke the interdependence between the passive-immediate and active-voluntary modes:

> In play, interest centers in activity, without much reference to its outcome. The sequence of deeds, images, emotions, suffices on its own account. In work, the end holds attention and controls the notice given to means. Since *the difference is one of direction of interest,* the contrast is one of emphasis, not of cleavage. When comparative prominence in consciousness of activity or outcome is transformed into isolation of one from the other, play degenerates into *fooling,* and work into *drudgery* [italics added]. (pp. 284–285)

Thus, Dewey (1933) thought that the optimal state for learning was to be "playful and serious at the same time" (p. 286), and modes of fooling and drudgery were detrimental to education.

This study refers to the playful–serious synchrony in the two directions of interest as *undivided interest*. Undivided interest, therefore, represents the combination of passive-immediate (i.e., playful) and active-voluntary (i.e., worklike) modes functioning in concert. *Divided interest,* on the other hand, refers to the disassociation of these two modes. Two kinds of divided interest can be distinguished: *Fooling* occurs when passive-immediate attention is used without the aid of active-voluntary attention to help direct the process. *Drudgery* occurs when active-voluntary attention is used without the spontaneity and emotional involvement afforded by passive-immediate attention.

James and Dewey believed that the rhythm between immediate and voluntary modes provided the intrinsic motion for learning and development. The alternation of spontaneous participation with a distancing to assess one's aims helped to keep interest organized and on track. However, neither thinker spent much time considering the experiential correlates of this dialectic. In other words, how does it feel when one is in balance or out of balance? How might such a balance be measured?

Csikszentmihalyi's (1990) flow model articulates in greater detail the dynamics of such a balance in subjective experience, and his development, with Larson, of the Experience Sampling Method (ESM) provided a means for investigating it in real contexts. Csikszentmihalyi conceptualized this dialectic of attention in terms of keeping skills and challenges in balance. These terms can be related to the passive-immediate/active-voluntary distinction in the following way. Skills are second-nature habits that allow automatic attention. For instance, when an expert pianist plays a piece of music, many dimensions of the performance do not require attention because of past experience and practice. The attention "saved" can be used to engage the challenges that introduce novelty and require a more active focusing of attention. By continually adjusting the balance between skills and challenges one regulates optimal arousal and maintains a person–environment fit that triggers optimal experience and motivates development (see Csikszentmihalyi & Rathunde, 1998).

Studies of talented adolescents and creative adults have provided strong support for the notion that undivided interest, or a synchrony of passive-immediate and active-voluntary attention, facilitates learning and skill development, and divided interest creates a negative impasse (see Csikszentmihalyi, Rathunde, & Whalen, 1997; Rathunde, 1993, 1995; Rathunde & Csikszentmihalyi, 1993; specific examples are discussed later in this article).

Family Support and Challenge and Adolescents' Undivided Interest: Findings From Cross-Sectional Studies

A number of cross-sectional studies have tried to integrate the ideas just discussed and explore the relation between adolescents' perceptions of the family context and their undivided interest (Rathunde, 1996). The link between family and experience that has been proposed in these studies is straightforward and consistent with broader themes in the literature on authoritative parenting and adolescence (Baumrind, 1989; Steinberg, 1990). Parents in a supportive family are seen by their children as warm and affectionate, listening in open and nonjudgmental ways, and helpful when the children are learning new skills or confronting obstacles. The assumption here is that when adolescents perceive such support they are more likely to engage in various activities in an unguarded, open, and spontaneous way (Rathunde, 1996). In a challenging family, on the other hand, parents are seen as modeling self-directed behavior, setting rules and limits, and expecting the adolescent to take steps that will lead to individuation and goal achievement. Thus, a challenging context is one wherein adolescents perceive that they are being asked to focus their attention, be more objective, and formulate plans that accommodate changing expectations. Therefore, it is a context in which adolescents are more likely to direct their attention to reach important goals (Rathunde, 1996).

A family context that is perceived as supportive and challenging, then, because it facilitates both directions of interest, is one that is more likely to be associated with the synchrony of immediate and voluntary modes of attention in undivided interest. Such a balanced family, in addition, provides a context wherein optimal arousal is more likely to occur. This observation, although it is derived from a more phenomenologically oriented research tradition, is consistent with other perspectives on the fit between an adolescent and the challenge level in his or her environment (see Eccles et al., 1993; Lerner & Lerner, 1987). Repeated experience in a family will develop habits of attention that will be exercised outside of the home context (Reiss, 1981; Strage, 1998). Thus, adolescents from supportive and challenging families are also more likely to demonstrate immediate involvement and an ability to focus their attention on goals when they are at school, and adolescents from families perceived as permissive (support without challenge) or authoritarian (challenge without support) are more likely to manifest habits of divided interest.

Results from cross-sectional studies have provided support for these assumptions and hypotheses. For instance, the ESM was used to operationalize the two directions of interest: the passive-immediate mode was assessed with ESM items that measured an adolescent's positive mood and energy at the moment he or she was signaled, and the active-voluntary mode was assessed with ESM items that asked whether one's present efforts were important for achieving goals. In samples of talented adolescents (see Rathunde, 1996) and average adolescents from various socioeconomic and ethnic backgrounds (see Rathunde, Carroll, & Huang, 2000), results consistently showed (a) a relation between the perception of high family support and adolescents' positive moods and (b) a significant link between the perception of family challenge and adolescents' focus on important goals. Adolescents from families that combined high support with high challenge showed the most positive experiential and time-use patterns in school (e.g., more optimal experiences and undivided interest, time in homework, hobbies, extracurricular activities, etc.) and they had higher levels of talent development and achievement (Csikszentmihalyi et al., 1997). In contrast, adolescents from high-support and low-challenge families were more invested in passive leisure (e.g., television viewing) and other modes of fooling, and adolescents from low-support and high-challenge families spent large amounts of time on important school activities, but reported negative moods and more drudgery.

None of the preceding studies, however, assessed perceptions of the family context and adolescents' experience at more than one point in time. Thus, nothing could be concluded about the relation of family and experience with respect to the development of undivided interest. The longitudinal data in this study provided the opportunity to assess whether the relations observed in previous work would hold over time, grow stronger, or diminish. Three basic hypotheses were investigated. First, it was expected that the relation between high family support and positive moods, and high family challenge and a focus on goals, would hold over time; that is, family conditions in Year 1 would predict adolescents' quality of experience in Year 3. Second, it was expected that the combination of high support and high challenge in Year 1 would be linked with undivided interest in Year 3, and that the permissive and authoritarian family extremes in Year 1 would be linked to patterns of divided interest in Year 3. Finally, it was hypothesized that increases in family support between Years 1 and 3 would be linked to increases in adolescents' moods over the same period, and that increases in family challenge would be linked to increases in the focus on important goals.

Methods

Participants

Data came from students who participated in two waves of data collection (1992–1993 and 1994–1995)

in the Alfred P. Sloan Study of Youth and Social Development (see Csikszentmihalyi & Schneider, 2000). The overall study collected information using interviews and surveys from 6th, 8th, 10th, and 12th graders from 33 elementary and secondary schools located at 12 sites across the United States. Selections of these sites optimized variations in labor force composition and participation, race and ethnicity, urbanicity, geographic location, and student ability level (for further details of the sampling design and procedures, see Csikszentmihalyi & Schneider, 2000). A focal sample of representative students responded to the ESM. Those with family information and ESM information in the first and second waves of the study comprise the present sample ($N = 247$). Three age cohorts (27% moved from Grade 6 to Grade 8; 42% from Grade 8 to Grade 10, and 31% from Grade 10 to Grade 12) and four ethnic groups (69% of the adolescents were White, 11% were Hispanic, 13% were African American, and 7% were Asian American) were studied. Adolescent boys comprised 38% of the sample and girls were 62%.

Procedure

Data collection in the first wave of the study proceeded over a period from late winter to early summer 1993. A team of trained interviewers went out to each site over a 2-week period and held orientations for focal students on responding to the ESM and other questionnaire protocols, most importantly the Teenage Life Questionnaire (i.e., a 50-page survey modified from the 1988 National Educational Longitudinal Study). Information about family support and challenge came from the Teenage Life Questionnaire. After completing the questionnaire, students were given watches that were programmed to randomly signal them eight times daily (7:30 a.m. to 10:30 p.m.) for 1 week. After being signaled, students recorded pertinent experiential information in a corresponding booklet of self-report forms with open-ended and scaled items. Two years later, students again answered questions about family support and challenge and responded to the ESM. Only students who completed at least 15 ESM self-reports for the week (in both waves) were included in the study. For additional reliability and validity information on the ESM method, see Csikszentmihalyi and Larson (1987).

Measures

Family support and challenge. The family measure was included in the Teenage Life Questionnaire and was comprised of 32 items that were designed to measure adolescents' perceptions of support and challenge in the home environment. The measure was created by the author based on modifications to the original measure (see Rathunde, 1996). The construct validity of the original measure has been supported in previous research by:

1. Comparisons to other family questionnaires.
2. Information provided by parents.
3. A pattern of differential results associated with support and challenge (see Rathunde, 1996).

The modified instrument clarified some of the original 24 items and added 8 new items in an attempt to more reliably measure the two family constructs.

Items on the family questionnaire measured support and challenge separately on a bipolar agree or disagree scale. With regard to support, for instance, adolescents either agreed or disagreed with statements like "In my family I feel appreciated for who I am" or "We enjoy having dinner together and talking." With regard to challenge, they agreed or disagreed with statements like "In my family I am expected to do my best" or "We express our opinions about current events, even when they differ." Items were phrased in positive and negative ways, and they addressed the family system as a whole. Guided by the past use of the questionnaire and by factor analyses using tetrachoric correlations on the entire sample in Year 1 (see Rathunde et al., 2000), 16 of the questionnaire items were summed to create one index of perceived familial support ($M = 6.1$, $SD = 3.8$, $\alpha = .81$), and the other 16 items were summed to measure family challenge ($M = 6.8$, $SD = 3.2$, $\alpha = .74$).

The correlation between the two factors was moderately high, $r = .65$. This correlation raised the possibility that only one dimension of families was being measured. However, a number of analyses in previous studies demonstrated that this was not the case. Results using these measures have consistently shown that the two family dimensions predict different outcomes in theoretically consistent ways, including different time use and experiential patterns (see Rathunde, 1996; Rathunde et al., 2000). If measures of support and challenge were capturing the same aspect of a family system, they would not be associated with different outcomes.

To create a balanced family typology, the support and challenge indexes were split at their medians within each grade cohort. This yielded four family types: high support/high challenge, high support/low challenge, low support/high challenge, and low support/low challenge.[1] The number of students within each family type

varied according to the response rate for various outcome variables (see Results).

ESM measures of mood and goal importance.

Factor analyses of the full set of ESM items revealed several factors (see Csikszentmihalyi & Schneider, 2000), two of which were used in this study because they best captured the immediate and goal-directed aspects of undivided attention. Mood was a composite variable based on seven semantic differential items relating to adolescents' momentary affect and feelings of energy (range = 1–7): excited, relaxed, happy, strong, active, sociable, and proud ($\alpha = .90$). Importance was a composite based on two items relating to the meaningfulness and focus of the activity (range = 1–9): "Was this activity important to you" and "How important was this activity to your overall goals," $r = .69$. In this study, measures of mood and importance were obtained by aggregating an adolescent's responses for the entire week of ESM participation in Years 1 and 3. For instance, if Student A responded to 30 signals for the week, average mood and importance would be created by averaging the 30 responses (Year 1 mood: $M = 4.8$, $SD = .76$; Year 1 importance: $M = 4.6$, $SD = 1.5$; Year 3 mood: $M = 4.6$, $SD = .64$; Year 3 importance: $M = 4.7$, $SD = 1.3$). After aggregating, z scores were created to eliminate scaling differences and to facilitate comparisons between the family groups (i.e., a mood or importance score of 0 would indicate an average score for the adolescent group).

ESM measures of undivided interest.

The separate measures of mood and goal importance were used in tandem to create four interest quadrants that highlighted various states of undivided or divided interest in Years 1 and 3. First, every ESM signal responded to by the adolescents was categorized based on whether it was high or low (i.e., above or below average or 0 using z scores) with respect to mood and importance; this resulted in four experiential quadrants (i.e., high mood/high importance, high mood/low importance, low mood/high importance, and low mood/low importance). Next, the percentage of time each adolescent spent in each experiential state was calculated. For instance, if an adolescent responded to the ESM 40 times, and 10 signals fell into each of the four categories, the adolescent would receive a score of 25% in each category. Because the ESM sampled approximately 100 hr of time, each percentage point is roughly equivalent to 1 hr of time (see Csikszentmihalyi et al., 1997).

Changes in family support and challenge.

Some of the analyses assessed the impact of changes in family support or challenge. Measures of change

---

[1] The means and standard deviations for support and challenge within each family group were as follows: high support ($M = 9.5$, $SD = 1.3$)/high challenge ($M = 9.7$, $SD = 1.2$), high support ($M = 8.2$, $SD = 1.1$)/low challenge ($M = 5.6$, $SD = 1.7$), low support ($M = 4.6$, $SD = 2.2$)/high challenge ($M = 8.7$, $SD = .8$), low support ($M = 2.5$, $SD = 3.0$)/low challenge ($M = 3.7$, $SD = 2.4$).

were created by subtracting Year 1 levels of each family variable from Year 3 levels. Negative values, therefore, indicated decreasing support or challenge by Year 3, whereas positive values indicated increasing support or challenge. Because adolescents' assessments of family support and family challenge both decreased slightly over the 2-year period, when no change occurred between Year 1 and Year 3 an adolescent's score was in the upper half of the distribution of change scores. Thus, no change can be interpreted as positive within the context of the sample and, therefore, was classified as increasing support or challenge. (Only 12% of the adolescent reports about their families indicated no change from Year 1 to Year 3.) Based on these values, a modified family typology was created. By Year 3, families were categorized as increasing support/increasing challenge (n = 86), increasing support/decreasing challenge (n = 35), decreasing support/increasing challenge (n = 52), and decreasing support/decreasing challenge (n = 74).

Changes in the quality of interest. Year 1 averages for mood and goal importance were subtracted from Year 3 averages to compute the change scores for these variables. In addition, Year 1 time percentages for the various interest quadrants were subtracted from Year 3 percentages. For all of these variables, negative values indicated decreasing interest and positive values indicated a growth in interest.

Background variables. Other questions on the Teenage Life Questionnaire provided information on the background variables of gender, grade (6, 8, 10, or 12), ethnicity (Asian American, African American, Hispanic, or White), and parental education (ranging from 1 [*less than high school*] to 7 [*PhD, MD, or other professional degree*]). Some missing values for parental education were estimated from other socioeconomic variables (i.e., social class and mean education levels in the parents' community).

Overview of the Analyses

The longitudinal analyses were divided into two parts, and each part addressed a different set of questions about the family context and adolescent experience. In Part 1, Year 1 measures of family support and challenge were related to the quality of adolescent experience in Year 3. These analyses helped to address the following questions: Was family support still related to adolescents' good moods? Was family challenge still associated with adolescents' focus on important goals? Was the balance of support and challenge (i.e., an authoritative family) still associ-

ated with undivided interest? Was an imbalance of support and challenge (i.e., permissive or authoritarian family types) still linked to divided interest? A key aspect of these analyses was to control for Year 1 levels of experience, as well as other relevant covariates, to test whether the family variables predicted changes in adolescents' quality of experience over and above any differences that occurred in the first year of the study.

Whereas the first set of analyses looked at changes in experience based on the original classification of the family context, the second set looked at how changes in the family context were related to changes in experience over the 2-year period. In other words, did a rise in family support or a rise in family challenge predict a corresponding increase in moods and importance?

Data analysis. The first set of analyses used multivariate analyses of covariance (MANCOVAs) to look at Year 3 experiences of interest based on the family classifications in Year 1. The MANCOVAs jointly controlled for six covariates using Bonferroni confidence intervals: grade, gender, parent education, and three ethnicity variables (i.e., Hispanic, Asian American, and African American; White was the comparison group). By holding constant these structural variables that differentiated families, any results presumably reflected the inner dynamics of the family rather than external factors associated with it. After assessing whether Year 1 family classifications were related to Year 3 experience, the MANCOVAs were repeated, this time adjusting for Year 1 quality of experience. If the results showed that the family context was still significantly related to the experiential outcomes, it would suggest that the family had an impact on the development of interest over and above any differences that were already present in Year 1.

The second set of analyses was designed to assess how changes in the family related to changes in experience over the 2-year period. To reliably capture these variations, a method was required that (a) simultaneously looked at changes in experience and the family context and (b) would adjust for regression to the mean effects on both measures (i.e., the natural movement of extremely high or low scores in Year 1 toward a more moderate position in Year 3). It was also helpful for theoretical purposes to retain a typological format in the analyses to allow for the testing of separate effects for family support, family challenge, and their interaction. Therefore, Part 2 of the analyses used MANCOVAs to compare the change scores for interest based on change scores for family support and challenge (see Measures). In other words, the MANCOVAs assessed changes in interest based on the modified family typology.[2]

All of the analyses in Part 2 controlled for Year 1 levels of family support, family challenge, and quality of interest. Together, the use of change scores and these covariates helped guard against regression or response biases that could have distorted the analyses. To conserve degrees of freedom, additional covariates were added on the basis of preliminary analyses. That is, if gender, grade, parental education, or ethnic background were related to observed changes in the quality of the family context or adolescent experience, they were included in the analyses.

Results

Year 3 Quality of Interest by Family Type in Year 1

Table 1 reports the results from the first set of analyses that compared family support and challenge levels in Year 1 and adolescents' experiential reports in Year 3. The first column of F values in Table 1 reports the relations between family context in Year 1 and adolescents' quality of interest in Year 3 before adjusting for the adolescents' interest in Year 1. The second column of F values in Table 1 reports the same relations after adjusting for Year 1 experience.

Interest dimensions before adjusting for Year 1 experience. After adjusting jointly for the covariates of gender, parental education, ethnicity, and grade level, there was a main effect for family support on adolescents' moods, $F(1, 273) = 4.90, p < .05$: Adolescents who perceived more family support in Year 1 reported higher moods in Year 3. There was no main effect for challenge and no interaction between support and challenge.

A contrasting effect, as expected, was found with respect to the family context and important goals. After adjusting for the covariates, there was a main effect for family challenge on goal importance, $F(1, 273) = 4.75$, $p < .05$; that is, adolescents who reported more family challenge in Year 1 reported a stronger focus on important goals in Year 3. There was no main effect for family support on goal importance, and there was no interaction between the two family dimensions.

Significant covariate findings ($p < .05$) revealed that older students reported less positive moods for the week, and African American students reported more positive moods than White students.[3] Covariate findings for importance showed that Hispanic students reported more goal importance than White students. None of the other covariates were significant.

Interest dimensions after adjusting for Year 1 experience. After adjusting for levels of mood and goal importance in Year 1, the main effects just discussed disappeared. That is, the variance in quality of experience that differentiated the family groups in Year 3 disappeared when adjusting for the variation in experience that was already present in Year 1. There was some indication that higher family support in Year 1 was related to reports of lower goal importance in Year 3, $F(1, 238) = 3.22, p = .07$. Covariate results ($p < .05$) showed that higher levels of mood and goal importance in Year 1 were significantly related to reports of higher levels in Year 3. Controlling for these experiential differences slightly changed the effects of the other covariates. African American students still reported higher moods in Year 3; in addition, older adolescents and adolescents with more highly educated parents reported more goal importance in Year 3.

Interest quadrants before adjusting for Year 1 experience. MANCOVAs were also used to assess the four interest quadrants. With respect to the high mood/high importance quadrant (i.e., undivided interest), after adjusting jointly for the covariates there was a main effect for family support on adolescents' undivided interest, $F(1, 272) = 3.76, p < .05$: Adolescents who perceived more support at home in Year 1 reported more undivided interest in Year 3. There was no main effect for challenge and no interaction between support and challenge.

For the second interest quadrant, or high mood/low importance (i.e., fooling), a main effect was found for family support, $F(1, 272) = 10.12, p < .01$: Adolescents who perceived more support at home in Year 1 reported more fooling in Year 3. There was a near-significant trend with respect to family challenge, $F(1, 272) = 3.58$, $p < .08$: Adolescents who perceived more challenge at home in Year 1 reported less fooling in Year 3. There was no interaction between support and challenge.

The strongest effects were found for the low mood/high importance quadrant (i.e., drudgery). There

---

[2]An alternative approach to data analysis would have been to combine the change analyses with the first set of MANCOVAs (i.e., enter the change scores for support and challenge as additional covariates in later steps of the analyses). Retaining the typological format for increases and decreases in support and challenge, however, was thought to have theoretical advantages for interpreting the findings and making comparisons to earlier studies.

---

[3]All covariate findings reported for a particular ethnic group reflect comparisons to White adolescents. In general, main effects for race and ethnicity are found in many analyses. Although they are not the focus of this study, future research might explore the relations between race and ethnicity and the family process measures.

Table 1. *Adolescents' Quality of Interest in Year 3 by Family Type in Year 1*

Quality of Experience	Family Type					F Values	
	High Support/ High Challenge	High Support/ Low Challenge	Low Support/ High Challenge	Low Support/ Low Challenge		Before Adjusting for Year 1 Experience	After Adjusting for Year 1 Experience
Interest Dimensions							
Momentary Mood	.11	.12	−.29	−.06	Support	4.90**	.13
					Challenge	.83	.64
					Support × Challenge	.75	1.91
Goal Importance	.08	−.14	.25	−.12	Support	.54	3.22*
					Challenge	4.75**	.28
					Support × Challenge	.33	.19
Interest Quadrants							
Undivided	26	24	17	22	Support	3.76**	.65
High Mood/					Challenge	.38	1.32
High Importance					Support × Challenge	2.00	.55
Fooling	20	22	12	18	Support	10.12***	4.28**
High Mood/					Challenge	3.58*	2.09
Low Importance					Support × Challenge	.55	3.22*
Drudgery	25	24	39	24	Support	7.72***	3.34*
Low Mood/					Challenge	9.13***	5.00**
High Importance					Support × Challenge	6.65***	5.65**
Disinterest	29	30	32	36	Support	2.39	.13
Low Mood/					Challenge	.71	.05
Low Importance					Support × Challenge	.22	.01

Note: The first column of *F* values results from 2 × 2 Multivariate Analyses of Covariance (high/low support by high/low challenge) that adjust jointly for the covariates: gender, parental education, ethnicity, and grade. The second column of *F* values reports findings after adjusting, in addition, for experience in year 1. Reported means for the interest dimensions are standardized Experience Sampling Method (ESM) variables; .00 is average for the adolescent group. Numbers for the interest quadrants are percentages of ESM beeps; for instance, 26 means 26% of time for the week was spent in that experiential state. All reported means are adjusted for the covariates.
*$p < .08$. **$p < .05$. ***$p < .01$.

was a main effect for family support, $F(1, 272) = 7.72$, $p < .01$: Adolescents who perceived more support at home in Year 1 reported less drudgery in Year 3. There was a main effect for family challenge, $F(1, 272) = 9.13$, $p < .01$: Adolescents who perceived more challenge at home in Year 1 reported more drudgery in Year 3. Finally, there was also an interaction between support and challenge, $F(1, 272) = 6.65$, $p < .01$. The combination of low support and high challenge in Year 1 led to the highest amounts of drudgery in Year 3. No significant effects were found for the disinterest quadrant (i.e., low moods/low importance).

Covariate findings indicated the following ($p < .05$): African American students reported more time spent in undivided interest, older students reported less fooling, older students and girls reported more time spent in drudgery, and African American students reported less time in this quadrant. Finally, African American students reported less time in the disinterest quadrant.

Interest quadrants after adjusting for Year 1 experience. In contrast to the findings for the mood and goal dimensions of interest, after adjusting for Year 1 levels in the particular interest quadrants,

the family context had an impact on adolescent experience over and above the differences already present in the first year of the study. This was the case for the fooling and drudgery quadrants. For instance, adolescents who reported more family support in Year 1 reported more fooling in Year 3, $F(1, 232) = 4.28$, $p < .05$. There was no effect for family challenge, and there was a near-significant interaction between support and challenge, $F(1, 232) = 3.22$, $p < .08$: Adolescents from low support/high challenge families reported the lowest amount of time in the fooling quadrant 2 years later.

After adjusting for time spent in the drudgery quadrant in Year 1, there was a near-significant effect for family support: Adolescents who felt more support in Year 1 reported less drudgery in Year 3, $F(1, 232) = 3.34$, $p < .08$. Adolescents who reported more family challenge in Year 1 reported more drudgery in Year 3, $F(1, 232) = 5.00$, $p < .05$. Also, there was a significant interaction between support and challenge, $F(1, 232) = 5.65$, $p < .05$: The combination of low support and high challenge in Year 1 led to the highest reported levels of drudgery 2 years later. Time estimates based on the ESM percentages suggest that adolescents in this family group spent about 15 hr more in this quadrant than teens in all other groups.

165

For all four quadrants, covariate findings ($p < .05$) suggested that time spent in a quadrant in Year 1 was positively related to time spent in that quadrant 2 years later. In other words, higher amounts of undivided interest, fooling, or drudgery in Year 1 predicted higher amounts in Year 3. Older students and Hispanic students spent more time in the drudgery quadrant, and African American students reported less time in this quadrant. Finally, older students and girls spent less time in the disinterest quadrant.

Specified contrasts for undivided and divided interest. A few a priori contrasts were specified in conjunction with the hypotheses about the family context and the development of undivided and divided interest. All of the contrasts reported here jointly controlled for the covariates.

As predicted, compared to adolescents in the other three groups, adolescents who reported high support and high challenge in Year 1 reported the highest amounts of undivided interest (26% of ESM signals) in Year 3, $t = 1.98$ ($p = .02$, one-tailed). However, this contrast was not significant after controlling for Year 1 time in the quadrant.

Hypotheses also predicted that the two extreme family types (i.e., permissive or high support/low challenge, and authoritarian or low support/high challenge) would manifest two different kinds of divided interest: fooling and drudgery, respectively. These hypotheses were tested with contrasts between these two groups. Adolescents from high support/low challenge families in Year 1 reported more fooling in Year 3 than adolescents from the low support/high challenge group, $t = 2.99$ ($p < .01$, one-tailed). This contrast retained significance after adjusting, in addition, for Year 1 time in the quadrant, $t = 2.09$ ($p = .02$, one-tailed). Conversely, adolescents from low support/high challenge families in Year 1 reported more drudgery in Year 3 than adolescents from the high support/low challenge group, $t = -3.42$ ($p < .001$, one-tailed). This contrast also retained significance after adjusting for Year 1 time in the drudgery quadrant, $t = -2.42$ ($p < .01$, one-tailed). These findings are depicted in Figure 1.

Change Analyses

Table 2 reports the results from the second set of analyses that compared changes in family support and challenge to changes in adolescents' reports of mood and importance across the 2 years of the study. All analyses in this section controlled for Year 1 levels of experience, family support, and family challenge. Preliminary analyses were used to determine which additional covariates were added to the analyses.

Interest dimensions. Results of the first MANCOVA indicated that an increase in family support was related to an increase in momentary mood, $F(1, 238) = 3.74$, $p = .05$; that is, adolescents who reported higher family support in Year 3 (compared to their Year 1 levels) also reported an increase in their moods over Year 1. There was no main effect for challenge and no interaction between support and challenge.

With respect to important goals, there were no main effects for family support and family challenge. However, there was a significant interaction between these two variables, $F(1, 238) = 4.35$, $p < .05$. The combination of increasing support with increasing challenge led to the highest increase in goal importance (+.13), and the combination of decreasing support with increasing challenge led to the largest decline in goal importance (−.16).

Covariate findings ($p < .05$) indicated that adolescents who reported lower moods and goal importance in Year 1 were more likely to report increases for both variables in Year 3.[4] The only other relevant covariate was parental education: Adolescents with more highly educated parents reported a significant increase in goal importance between Years 1 and 3.

Interest quadrants. Analyses for changes in the interest quadrants produced only one significant finding. There was an interaction between family support and challenge, $F(1, 235) = 4.19$, $p < .05$. Increases in

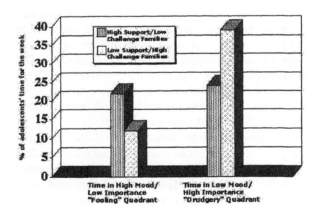

Figure 1. Amounts of fooling and drudgery in Year 3 by family type in Year 1.

---

[4]These findings confirm that there was some regression to the mean in Year 3. However, the use of change scores, and the fact that Year 1 levels of all the variables were entered as covariates in the analyses, helped guard against regression effects distorting the overall results.

Table 2. *Change in Adolescents' Quality of Interest by Change in Family Support and Challenge*

Change in Quality of Interest	Family Changes in Support and Challenge					F Values
	Increase Support/ Increase Challenge	Increase Support/ Decrease Challenge	Decrease Support/ Increase Challenge	Decrease Support/ Decrease Challenge		
Interest Dimensions						
Momentary Mood	.18	.07	−.20	−.00	Support	3.74**
					Challenge	.12
					Support × Challenge	1.97
Goal Importance	.13	−.09	−.16	.10	Support	.18
					Challenge	.02
					Support × Challenge	4.35**
Interest Quadrants						
Undivided	3.3	−1.1	−4.3	.8	Support	1.33
High Mood/					Challenge	.02
High Importance					Support × Challenge	4.19**
Fooling	−.7	.2	−1.6	−5.3	Support	2.80*
High Mood/					Challenge	.49
Low Importance					Support × Challenge	1.58
Drudgery	1.6	1.7	2.2	5.8	Support	.79
Low Mood/					Challenge	.48
High Importance					Support × Challenge	.51
Disinterest	−3.4	−1.1	3.2	−1.2	Support	1.63
Low Mood/					Challenge	.16
Low Importance					Support × Challenge	1.94

Note: The F values result from 2 × 2 Multivariate Analyses of Covariance (high/low support by high/low challenge) that adjust jointly for experience in Year 1, family support and challenge in Year 1, and all other relevant covariates. Reported means for the interest dimensions are standardized Experience Sampling Method (ESM) variables; .00 is average for the adolescent group. Numbers for the interest quadrants are percentages of ESM beeps; for instance, 3.3 means a 3.3% increase of time in that experiential state across the 2-year measurement period. All reported means are adjusted for the covariates.

*$p < .08$. **$p < .05$.

support and challenge led to the largest increase in time spent in the high mood/high importance quadrant (+3.3%, or about 3 hr), whereas the combination of decreasing support and increasing challenge led to the largest decline in undivided interest (−4.3%, or about 4 hr). There also was a near-significant trend indicating that increases in family support were associated with increases in amount of time in the fooling quadrant, $F(1, 235) = 2.80, p < .08$.

Covariate findings ($p < .05$) indicated that adolescents with lower percentages in a quadrant were more likely to report an increase in that quadrant 2 years later (see footnote 4). Hispanic adolescents were more likely to report a decline in undivided interest, African American students reported a decline in time spent in the low mood/high importance (drudgery) quadrant, and older adolescents reported less time in the low mood/low importance (disinterest) quadrant.

Specified contrasts for undivided and divided interest. The contrast between adolescents in the increasing support/increasing challenge family group versus the other three groups (jointly controlling for experience in Year 1 and other relevant covariates)

suggested that this family group was optimal for the growth of undivided interest, $t = 1.96$ ($p < .05$, one-tailed). The contrasts between the extreme family groups (i.e., increasing support/decreasing challenge and decreasing support/increasing challenge) showed no significant results with respect to changes in divided interest.

Discussion

Comparing the findings across the two sets of analyses provides insights beyond those that either set would provide in isolation. The first set of analyses (Year 1 to Year 3) addresses how various combinations of family support and challenge in Year 1 are linked to adolescents' moods and goals 2 years later, and whether, after adjusting for experiential differences in Year 1, the family typology can predict the development of interest above and beyond any differences that occurred in Year 1. The change analyses, in contrast, explore how increasing and decreasing levels of support and challenge affect changes in adolescents' quality of interest, regardless of the levels of family support and challenge that were present in Year 1. Comparisons across both sets of analyses, therefore, will help sort out the importance of the continuity of family support and challenge (i.e., past levels in the family), the importance of change from Year 1 to Year 3, and how continuity and change in the family may have contributed to the development of undivided interest.

Continuity and Change in the Family and Undivided Interest

The results confirmed that levels of family support and challenge in Year 1 could predict adolescents' momentary moods and focus on important goals 2 years later. Consistent with earlier cross-sectional studies (see Rathunde, 1996; Rathunde et al., 2000), higher family support was again related to adolescents' positive moods, and higher family challenge was associated with a stronger focus on goals. These findings add the dimension of time to earlier work and demonstrate that after 2 years these two dimensions of family dynamics are still empirically linked to these different facets of interest. The fact that adjusting for Year 1 levels of mood and the importance of goals made these results disappear, however, suggests that the type of family context did not predict the development of interest beyond the differences that were already present in the first year of the study. Unexpectedly, family support in Year 1 was negatively related to Year 3 goals, but this finding was only marginally significant.

A different story emerged with the results for the interest quadrants. The quadrants did not measure mood and goals separately; instead, they assessed how much time adolescents spent in various high and low combinations of the two variables, or how much time they spent in states of undivided or divided interest. Results for these interest variables showed that the quality of the family context in Year 1 predicted time differences in the interest quadrants 2 years later, even after adjusting for adolescents' interest levels in Year 1. More specifically, the type of family context in Year 1 predicted the development of divided interest, or times when moods and goals were disassociated.

The most interesting of these differences occurred in relation to adolescents from families who provided low support with high challenge in Year 1. Adolescents from this family group reported the lowest amount of time in the fooling quadrant. If each percentage point is seen as an approximation of 1 hr of time, adolescents from low support/high challenge families spent about 6 to 10 hr less than adolescents from other families in the "fooling around" state of feeling good but not focusing on anything important. Even more striking were the findings for the drudgery quadrant. Adolescents from low-support and high-challenge families reported spending about 15 hr more per week in drudgery. This experiential quadrant clearly represented their highest time investment, and it suggests a time-use pattern of substantial importance that is likely to have a negative impact on the lives of these adolescents.

The adolescents most likely to spend time in undivided interest were those from high-support/high-challenge families. Those most likely to spend time in the fooling quadrant were from high-support/low-challenge families, and those most likely to spend time in the disinterest quadrant were from low-support/low-challenge families. Although adolescents from all of the family groups spent fairly large amounts of time in disinterest, it must be remembered that the quadrant percentages reflect time use for the entire week. Therefore, it includes all of the "down time" and maintenance activities (e.g., combing hair, getting ready to go somewhere, driving somewhere, etc.) that adolescents engage in during a typical week.

The interest quadrant findings are important because they indicate that levels of family support and challenge from previous years had a developmental impact on adolescents' quality of experience. The change analyses added information on how experience was affected by increases or decreases in family support and challenge. These findings showed that adolescents who perceived an increase in support over the 2-year period also reported a rise in their moods. Although it was expected that the same one-to-one relation would hold between family challenge and goals, the findings indicate that it was the interaction of changing levels of support and challenge that was most relevant for goals. In other words, the mixed messages of increasing support and decreasing challenge, and decreasing support and increasing challenge, led to the largest declines in adolescents' concentration on goals.

It is reasonable to assume that the decreasing focus on goals for these two family groups occurred for very different reasons. Perhaps adolescents in the former family group (increasing support/decreasing challenge) were losing confidence in their goals because they were getting the message that other family members thought they needed help and they did not really expect much from them, whereas those from the decreasing support/increasing challenge group might have been receiving the message that more and more was expected but support could not be counted on. Adolescents in the latter predicament might have felt overwhelmed by the demands being placed on them, or perhaps they were starting to resent these demands and were tuning them out. Whatever the reason, this group of adolescents reported the largest decline in goals (−.16). On the other hand, when parents increased challenges and, at the same time, increased their support, adolescents reported the largest increase in the focus on goals (+.13).

There was only one significant finding when looking at changes in the family and changes in the interest quadrants. However, the one interaction was important in that it addressed the development of undivided interest. Adolescents from families who reported an increase in both support and challenge reported spending about 3 hr more a week in undivided interest. Increasing family support and challenge presumably helped the adolescents to feel more open to experience and more focused; therefore, it increased the probability for those times when these two directions of interest were in synchrony. In contrast, those who reported decreasing support and increasing challenge spent about 4 hr less in undivided interest. Because this mode of experience represents times when adolescents are genuinely engaged—both at the moment and for long-term reasons—it is reasonable to assume that 3 or 4 hr a week could have a substantial developmental impact.

The following tentative conclusions might be reached when looking across the two sets of findings. Adolescents' perceptions of family support and challenge had a stable effect on their moods and goals, but not a developmental one. In other words, differences in moods and goals that were present in Year 3 were already present in Year 1, or Year 3 differences in moods and goals were related to changes in the perceptions of family support and challenge that occurred over the 2 years of the study. However, when looking at the combined influence of moods and goals in terms of the interest quadrants, several findings suggested that perceptions of the family in Year 1 did affect the later ability to synchronize passive-immediate and active-voluntary modes in undivided interest. That is, even after adjusting for the interest quadrant differences that were already present in Year 1, adolescents from overly supportive and overly challenging families showed a progression toward the disassociation of positive moods and important goals. Two years later it seemed that Year 1 conditions in the family were having a continuing impact on the experiential modes of fooling and drudgery.

The pragmatic message for parents, therefore, is mixed. On the one hand, the findings suggest that differences in a family that affect adolescents' quality of experience can be changed, and these changes can have a positive (or negative) impact on experience. On the other hand, some of the interest quadrant results suggest that damage done in the past will have mounting consequences a few years later, especially if a family is seen by an adolescent as highly demanding but not very supportive (see also Weiss & Schwarz, 1996, on the preponderance of negative outcomes associated with an authoritarian-directive type of family).

In general, this study adds further support to the notions that adolescents' perceptions of family support are related to their immediate moods, their perceptions of family challenge are linked to their long-term goals, and the combination of these two family dimensions is associated with undivided interest. These findings,

however, are limited in that they are based solely on self-reports. Future research should look at these relations with alternative methods (e.g., observations; see Rathunde, 1997) and should include more detailed information from parents.

An Experiential Perspective on the Development of Undivided Interest: Implications and Conclusions

The experiential findings in this study are consistent with a central theme in the adolescent literature: Adolescents benefit from a continued connection to the family while being challenged to develop their skills and individuality (Baumrind, 1989; Hauser, 1991; Steinberg, 1990; Weiss & Schwarz, 1996). Most of the research on this general theme, however, pays little attention to the experiential consequences of a family context. For instance, much is known about the positives of authoritative families and the negatives associated with permissive and authoritarian families, but how do adolescents experience their lives when they feel connected without being challenged (i.e., permissive families) or when they are being pushed too hard without feeling supported emotionally (i.e., authoritarian families)? Although the interrelations of socialization, optimal stimulation, and self-regulation are sometimes discussed (see, for instance, Lerner & Lerner, 1987; McIntyre & Dusek, 1995; Rogoff, 1990; Strage, 1998), an explicitly phenomenological approach is seldom taken, despite the fact that there is good empirical support for the hypothesis that optimal experience and interest have positive developmental benefits (Deci & Ryan, 1985; Rathunde & Csikszentmihalyi, 1993; Renninger, Hidi, & Krapp, 1992).

A few previous studies have looked at the interrelations between adolescents' perceptions of their family and their quality of experience and interest (see Rathunde, 1996, 1997; Rathunde et al., 2000). Results in these studies have identified unique experiential profiles associated with permissive and authoritarian families, and a pattern of optimal experience (e.g., flow and undivided interest) and achievement associated with the combination of support and challenge. However, this work has looked at the relation between the family and experience at one point in time. Therefore, it could not answer questions about experiential habits that may or may not be developing in connection with the family. It is only with this longitudinal study that a broader perspective can be taken on the development of undivided interest.

As parents exert less of an immediate impact on an adolescent's life, the possibility of lifelong learning becomes increasingly dependent on the adolescent's capacity for sustaining his or her interest through self-regulation. Most researchers would agree that it is important to explore how parents can facilitate the development of this capacity. However, few would place an experiential perspective at or near the center of such exploration. To appreciate what such a perspective might offer depends, arguably, on how much value one places on the quality of subjective experience and the notion of undivided interest. Three ideas have led to the strong emphasis placed on undivided interest in this study:

1. There are two basic modes of attention that must work together to sustain interest: One is a passive-immediate mode of attention and the other is a more active-voluntary mode (James, 1890).

2. Habits of separating these two ways of engaging the world will disrupt interest and the potential for lifelong learning (Dewey, 1913, 1938).

3. The synergistic coordination of both modes will result in more frequent optimal experiences that stimulate the development of skills (Csikszentmihalyi & Rathunde, 1998).

The usefulness of these ideas for understanding lifelong learning was recently illustrated by a study of approximately 90 eminent and creative adults (see Csikszentmihalyi, 1997; Rathunde, 1995). The individuals who were studied provided numerous anecdotes describing the particular combinations of heart and mind that kept their interests undivided and synergistic. They also provided vivid accounts of impasses in their work when immediate interest and long-term goals interfered with each other. One of the more memorable anecdotes was provided by historian Natalie Davis, who recalled a feeling of floating along with a project, yet also watching herself from a distance. She associated this mode of engagement with the highest enjoyment, and it was self-corrective. In other words, each of the two vantage points could correct for the other: The scholarly distance could prevent the blindness of immediate interest, and the exuberance of the moment could fight off the dryness of abstract ideas. Davis' comment is consistent with the Jamesian perspective on the coordination of immediate and voluntary modes, and it is reminiscent of the following comment: "The knower is an actor, ... on one side, whilst on the other he registers the truth which he helps to create" (James, 1960, p. 28).

Such mature forms of undivided interest are beyond the capacities of adolescents. However, a precursor to these mature self-regulatory styles may already be present in adolescents' abilities to coordinate their immediate moods with their important goals. If so, this study suggests something important about how a family facilitates a flexibility of mind that helps adolescents coordinate their attention and develop habits of undivided interest.

References

Avenevoli, S., Sessa, F., & Steinberg, L. (1999). Family structure, parenting practices, and adolescent adjustment: An ecological examination. In E. M. Hetherington (Ed.), *Coping with divorce, single parenting, and remarriage: A risk and resiliency perspective* (pp. 65–90). Mahwah, NJ: Lawrence Erlbaum Associates, Inc.

Baumrind, D. (1989). Rearing competent children. In W. Damon (Ed.), *Child development today and tomorrow* (pp. 349–378). San Francisco: Jossey-Bass.

Boyes, M., & Allen, S. (1993). Styles of parent–child interaction and moral reasoning in adolescence. *Merrill-Palmer Quarterly, 39,* 551–570.

Cooper, C. R., Grotevant, H. D., & Condon, S. M. (1983). Individuality and connectedness in the family as a context for adolescent identity formation and role-taking skill. In H. D. Grotevant & C. R. Cooper (Eds.), *Adolescent development in the family* (pp. 43–59). San Francisco: Jossey-Bass.

Csikszentmihalyi, M. (1990). *Flow: The psychology of optimal experience.* New York: Harper & Row.

Csikszentmihalyi, M. (1997). *Creativity: Flow and the psychology of discovery and invention.* New York: HarperCollins.

Csikszentmihalyi, M., & Larson, R. (1987). Validity and reliability of the experience-sampling method. *Journal of Nervous and Mental Disease, 175,* 526–536.

Csikszentmihalyi, M., & Rathunde, K. (1998). The development of the person: An experiential perspective on the ontogenesis of psychological complexity. In W. Damon (Series Ed.) & R. M. Lerner (Vol. Ed.), *Handbook of child psychology: Vol. 1. Theoretical models of human development* (pp. 635–684). New York: Wiley.

Csikszentmihalyi, M., Rathunde, K., & Whalen, S. (1997). *Talented teenagers: The roots of success and failure.* New York: Cambridge University Press.

Csikszentmihalyi, M., & Schneider, B. (2000). *Becoming adult.* New York: Basic Books.

Deci, E. L., & Ryan, R. M. (1985). *Intrinsic motivation and self-determination in human behavior.* New York: Plenum.

Dewey, J. (1913). *Interest and effort in education.* Cambridge, MA: Riverside.

Dewey, J. (1933). *How we think.* Boston: Heath.

Dewey, J. (1938). *Experience and education.* New York: Macmillan.

Eccles, J. S., Midgley, C., Wigfield, A., Buchanan, C. M., Reuman, D., Flanagan, C., & Mac Iver, D. (1993). Development during adolescence: The impact of stage–environment fit on young adolescents' experiences in schools and in families. *American Psychologist, 48,* 90–101.

Field, T. (1985). Attachment as psychobiological attunement: Being on the same wave length. In M. Reite & T. Field (Eds.), *Psychobiology of attachment* (pp. 415–454). Orlando, FL: Academic.

Freud, S. (1933). *New introductory lectures on psychoanalysis.* New York: Norton.

Hauser, S. (1991). *Adolescents and their families.* New York: Free Press.

Jackson, C., Henriksen, L., & Foshee, V. (1998). The Authoritative Parenting Index: Predicting health risk behaviors among children and adolescents. *Health Education and Behavior, 25,* 319–337.

James, W. (1890). *The principles of psychology.* New York: Dover.

James, W. (1960). What pragmatism means. In M. R. Konvitz & G. Kennedy (Eds.), *The American pragmatists* (pp. 28–44). Cleveland, OH: World.

Lamborn, S., Mounts, N., Steinberg, L., & Dornbusch, S. (1991). Patterns of competence and adjustment among adolescents from authoritative, authoritarian, indulgent, and neglectful families. *Child Development, 62,* 1049–1065.

Lerner, R., & Lerner, J. (1987). Children in their contexts: A goodness-of-fit model. In J. Lancaster, J. Altmann, A. Rossi, & L. Sherrod (Eds.), *Parenting across the life span* (pp. 377–404). New York: Aldine de Gruyter.

Mantzicopoulos, P., & Oh-Hwang, Y. (1998). The relationship of psychosocial maturity to parenting quality and intellectual ability for American and Korean adolescents. *Contemporary Educational Psychology, 23,* 195–206.

McIntyre, J., & Dusek, J. (1995). Perceived parental rearing practices and styles of coping. *Journal of Youth and Adolescence, 24,* 499–509.

Rathunde, K. (1993). The organization of energy in work and play: Dewey's philosophy of experience and the everyday lives of teenagers. *Society and Leisure, 16,* 59–76.

Rathunde, K. (1995). Wisdom and abiding interest: Interviews with three noted historians in later life. *Journal of Adult Development, 2,* 159–172.

Rathunde, K. (1996). Family context and talented adolescents' optimal experience in school-related activities. *Journal of Research on Adolescence, 6,* 603–626.

Rathunde, K. (1997). Parent–adolescent interaction and interest. *Journal of Youth and Adolescence, 26,* 669–689.

Rathunde, K., Carroll, M., & Huang, M. (2000). Families and the forming of children's occupational future. In M. Csikszentmihalyi & B. Schneider (Eds.), *Becoming adult* (pp. 113–139). New York: Basic Books.

Rathunde, K., & Csikszentmihalyi, M. (1993). Undivided interest and the growth of talent: A longitudinal study of adolescents. *Journal of Youth and Adolescence, 22,* 1–21.

Reiss, D. (1981). *The family's construction of reality.* Cambridge, MA: Harvard University Press.

Renninger, K. A., Hidi, S., & Krapp, A. (Eds.). (1992). *The role of interest in learning and development.* Hillsdale, NJ: Lawrence Erlbaum Associates, Inc.

Rogoff, B. (1990). *Apprenticeship in thinking: Cognitive development in social context.* New York: Oxford University Press.

Steinberg, L. (1990). Autonomy, conflict, and harmony in the family relationship. In S. Feldman & G. Elliot (Eds.), *At the threshold: The developing adolescent* (pp. 255–276). Cambridge, MA: Harvard University Press.

Steinberg, L., Lamborn, S., Dornbusch, S., & Darling, N. (1992). Impact of parenting practices on adolescent achievement: Authoritative parenting, school involvement, and encouragement to succeed. *Child Development, 63,* 1266–1281.

Steinberg, L., Mounts, N., Lamborn, S., & Dornbusch, S. (1991). Authoritative parenting and adolescent adjustment across varied ecological niches. *Journal of Research on Adolescence, 1,* 19–36.

Strage, A. (1998). Family context variables and the development of self-regulation in college students. *Adolescence, 33*(129), 17–31.

Taylor, L., Hinton, I., & Wilson, M. (1995). Parental influences on academic performance in African-American students. *Journal of Child and Family Studies, 4,* 293–302.

Walker, L. J., & Taylor, J. H. (1991). Family interactions and the development of moral reasoning. *Child Development, 62,* 264–283.

Weiss, L., & Schwarz, J. (1996). The relationship between parenting types and older adolescents' personality, academic achievement, adjustment, and substance use. *Child Development, 67,* 2101–2114.

Received December 14, 1999
Final revision received July 12, 2000
Accepted August 21, 2000

Applied Developmental Science
2001, Vol. 5, No. 3, 172–183

Family, School, and Community Predictors of Adolescent Growth-Conducive Experiences: Global and Specific Approaches

Joel M. Hektner

North Dakota State University

Using a diverse national sample of adolescents followed for 2 years, several models linking contextual and individual factors to adolescent growth-conducive experiences were tested. Adolescent autonomy, concentration, intrinsic motivation, and goal-directedness during productive activities were measured via the Experience Sampling Method, in which each participant provided multiple responses daily for 1 week in each of 2 years. Structural equation modeling was used to estimate relations among both specific aspects and global constructs of contextual or individual characteristics and experiential dimensions. Growth-conducive environment, as measured by the degree of support and challenge in the school and family, was found to be positively related concurrently to growth-conducive experiences and longitudinally to time spent engaged in productive activities. Autonomy during productive activities was also related to growth-conducive experiences and intrinsic motivation 2 years later. Results imply that teachers, parents, and communities can promote positive youth development by maintaining an environment rich in interpersonal support, autonomy, and opportunities to pursue challenges related to future goals.

The conditions of adolescents' experiences and social contexts that are most conducive to the development of their skills and talents have been the focus of a growing body of research (Adlai-Gail, 1994; Csikszentmihalyi & Larson, 1984; Csikszentmihalyi, Rathunde, & Whalen, 1993; Deci & Ryan, 1985; Hektner, 1996). These studies have laid the foundation for a comprehensive model of the process of talent development, or growth, in adolescence. In this theoretical model, adolescents' subjective experience of schoolwork and other productive activities plays a key role in mediating the relation between contextual characteristics and the development of new skills. That is, certain contextual characteristics are thought to influence talent development partly by means of their effects on how productive activities are subjectively experienced. This relation can be represented in a model with two sets of pathways, with one set linking features of context to dimensions of experience and another set linking those experiential dimensions to developmental outcomes. The purpose of this study is to

test the internal validity of a particular conception of growth-conducive experiences and to define and test the first half of this comprehensive model—that is, to model the relation between contextual characteristics and growth-conducive experiences.

The latter half of this model, linking a particular type of subjective experiences with talent development, has been demonstrated in work by Csikszentmihalyi (1988) and others on *flow,* optimal experiences in which individuals engage their skills in challenging activities, thereby feeling great enjoyment. The positive experience and intrinsic motivation associated with flow fuel a cycle in which people, after mastering one set of challenges, need to pursue new challenges requiring the development of more complex skills if they are to maintain their interest and enjoyment. In a study by Csikszentmihalyi et al. (1993), high school seniors who as freshmen had reported experiencing more flow during school activities developed their talents further than those who had reported less flow. Similarly, Hektner (1996) reported that adolescents who increased in flow over 2 years were further than their peers along the developmental pathway toward finding a productive role they were capable of and would enjoy.

This research was funded by Grant 92–10–1 from the Alfred P. Sloan Foundation, whose support is hereby gratefully acknowledged. However, the conclusions drawn here are those of the author and are not necessarily endorsed by the foundation.

Thanks are also due to Mihaly Csikszentmihalyi, Barbara Schneider, and the anonymous reviewers for their comments on drafts of this article.

Requests for reprints should be sent to Joel M. Hektner, Department of Child Development and Family Science, North Dakota State University, P.O. Box 5057, Fargo, ND 58105. E-mail: Joel_Hektner@ndsu.nodak.edu

Experiential Dimensions

In these instances, flow could be thought of as a growth-conducive experience. However, the flow experience per se may not always be conducive to positive development, because any activity can be associated with flow. Growth-conducive experiences, as conceptualized in this study, are flow experiences that occur during engagement in productive activities and include high levels of goal-directedness, concentration, and intrinsic motivation. Each of these three elements is an integral part of flow experiences in general, as described by Csikszentmihalyi (1988), and each plays a role in facilitating the development of new skills and talents. Goal-directedness in itself, like flow, is neutral with respect to positive development, because its role depends on the goals that are chosen. If adolescents develop goals pertaining to current productive activities and future productive roles, these goals will stimulate positive growth by providing a focus for their energies and a standard by which to evaluate their progress. The role of the second element, intense and focused concentration, is to sustain the flow experience so that full engagement of skills can occur. When adolescents focus their concentration on schoolwork or a useful hobby, they are likely to develop their skills and talents as they meet current challenges and pursue new ones. Finally, the positive experiential state associated with flow makes flow activities intrinsically motivating, so adolescents will want to allocate their energy and attention toward their goals (Hektner & Csikszentmihalyi, 1996). As their skills increase, adolescents will be led by their intrinsic motivation to pursue new and more difficult challenges, which will in turn facilitate further skill development. Thus, intrinsic motivation to engage in productive activities, when accompanied by concentration and goal-directedness, is thought to be conducive to significant talent development in adolescents.

This definition of growth-conducive experience represents an attempt to distill, within the broader class of flow experiences, just those elements that are most likely to contribute to development. Although the definition focuses on the qualitative aspects of experiences that make them conducive to development, the frequency or quantity of these experiences is limited by the amount of time adolescents spend engaged in the activities most likely to facilitate the growth of talent, namely, productive activities or active leisure pursuits such as sports or hobbies. Consequently, the endogenous, or dependent, variables tested in this model include the three qualitative elements of growth-conducive experience, both individually and collectively, and time spent engaged in productive activities and active leisure. The hypothesized predictors of these experiential variables are a set of individual and contextual characteristics (described later) that had separately been demonstrated in previous research to be associated with flow. Thus, the design and testing of this model is an effort both to integrate findings from separate studies into a comprehensive model and to refine the focus of this line of research.

Contextual and Individual Characteristics

Researchers have long recognized that development occurs within multiple contexts (Bronfenbrenner, 1979; Ford & Lerner, 1992); for adolescents these include families, schools, and communities. The largest body of research and the strongest findings appear to be on the role of the family. Rathunde (1996) found that adolescents who perceived high levels of both challenge and support in their families reported more optimal experience in schoolwork, as indicated by both spontaneity and goal-directedness. Members of such a family encourage their adolescent to develop an independent identity marked by unique and complex interests and skills. At the same time, they provide him or her with the security of belonging to a close network of supportive interpersonal relationships. These family qualities have been shown to be related to other positive developmental outcomes, including academic achievement (Lamborn, Mounts, Steinberg, & Dornbusch, 1991; Steinberg, Lamborn, Dornbusch, & Darling, 1992). Two indicators of a family that encourages the pursuit of challenges are a cognitively stimulating home environment and parents' educational aspirations for their children. In a longitudinal study that controlled for socioeconomic status (SES), Gottfried, Fleming, and Gottfried (1998) demonstrated that the former was related to academic intrinsic motivation, and in a separate study the latter was linked to children's school achievement (Gottfried, 1991). In the model considered here, indicators of support and challenge from the family are included as predictors of growth-conducive experiences.

As adolescents age, the social environment of the school becomes an increasingly important context for growth-conducive experiences. School has the potential to be the most consistent source of challenging opportunities and the most likely setting for skill development. Csikszentmihalyi et al. (1993) reported that the teachers most remembered by talented students for sparking their desire to learn were those who demonstrated abiding concern and tailored the level of challenges they offered to the skills of their students. These reflections are consistent with evidence from a study by Hektner (1997) in which support and challenge in the school setting were found to be significant predictors of adolescent flow experiences. Just as in the family context, the dimensions of support and challenge emerged as important features of the school environment in promoting growth-conducive experiences. Hence, school support and challenge are also included in the model presented here.

173

Another contextual variable that is included is autonomy, because it has received much attention for its role in promoting intrinsic motivation and flow (e.g., Deci, 1995; Wong, 1993). If adolescents feel that they are doing something because they have to, rather than because they want to, they are much less likely to experience flow (Wong, 1993). Although a sense of autonomy is in part determined by individual perceptual characteristics, numerous studies have shown how environmental conditions established by teachers and parents play a significant role in adolescents' perceptions of autonomy (Deci, 1992; Deci & Ryan, 1987; Noom & Dekovic, 1998; Silverberg & Gondoli, 1996). Thus, in addition to support and challenge, the family and school environments that best facilitate growth-conducive experiences appear to be those that also allow adolescents significant leeway in choosing and controlling their own activities.

Because of its role in enabling families to acquire resources and access to better schools, SES could also be plausibly hypothesized as a factor determining the opportunities an adolescent has for growth-conducive experiences. However, flow experiences have been reported by people across the socioeconomic spectrum (Csikszentmihalyi, 1990), and Adlai-Gail (1994) found no social class, gender, or racial differences among samples of adolescents with high and low levels of flow. The weakness (or lack) of the relation between flow and social class may be attributed to aspects of the social environment that do not correlate with SES. For example, in a study of talented adolescents by Csikszentmihalyi et al. (1993), there was no association between SES and levels of family support and challenge. Nevertheless, SES is included in the model presented here so that it can be tested once again.

In addition to these characteristics of the social contexts of adolescent development, researchers have also examined individual characteristics such as age and gender. Clearly, there is an inherent relation between age and development for normal adolescents, but in terms of growth-conducive experiences the change with age may involve the degree of challenges and skills involved rather than the quality of the subjective experience. Hektner (1996) found no overall change in frequency of flow over 2 years in a sample of 6th through 10th graders. Several studies have also reported a lack of gender differences in flow frequency (Adlai-Gail, 1994; Csikszentmihalyi & Larson, 1984; Hektner, 1996). In an effort to replicate or qualify these findings, both age and gender are included in this model.

Global and Specific Approaches

To summarize, the proposed model hypothesizes relations between a set of individual and contextual characteristics (support and challenge in the family and school, autonomy, SES, age, and gender) and a set of experiential dimensions (time spent in productive activities and in active leisure; and goal-directedness, intrinsic motivation, and concentration while engaged in productive activities). The elements within each of these sets can be thought of as independent aspects of context or experience, or they can be thought to combine synergistically into global constructs, such as the proposed combination of goal-directedness, concentration, and intrinsic motivation to produce growth-conducive experiences. Within the set of contextual characteristics, a global construct including support and challenge in the family and school can be proposed that would represent the growth-conducive environment produced by the simultaneous presence of these four elements.

To test the internal validity of these global constructs and to include both the constructs and the elements that comprise them into a comprehensive analysis, a structural equation modeling approach is used. This approach allows for the testing of the relations among both the specific elements and global constructs included in the model. The value of examining the relations among specific dimensions of context and experience is that both constructs are multifaceted. To understand more fully which contextual characteristics facilitate which dimensions of growth-conducive experiences, we need to tease apart these unique relations. On the other hand, given the strong associations among growth-conducive contextual characteristics and among positive dimensions of experience, there is also value in testing whether the specific dimensions combine into global constructs. This type of analysis would show, for example, whether any added benefit is derived from a combination of positive contextual dimensions beyond the additive effect of each one.

To accomplish these analytical objectives, three conceptual models were developed. In the first, every individual and contextual characteristic in the model was hypothesized to predict every experiential dimension. The second model included two latent constructs, unmeasured conceptual variables that capture the commonality among their measured indicators. One latent construct, growth-conducive environment, was designed to be indicated by the four support and challenge dimensions. The second, growth-conducive experience, was constructed with goal-directedness, intrinsic motivation, and concentration during productive activities as indicators. A significant pathway was hypothesized between these two constructs; this would demonstrate a relation between the global concepts they represent.

Both of these models were conceptualized as representing static relations within a given developmental period. As such, they are correlational in nature and could only suggest potential causal pathways. Although longitudinal models are also correlational in design, the a priori specification of relations between variables occurring earlier versus later in time sets up a more rigorous test of the underlying theory. The third conceptual model, an extension of the second across 2 years, was constructed to test the longer term relations between context and experience. Thus, contextual and individual variables at Year 1 were hypothesized to predict the same at Year 3 and experiential variables at Years 1 and 3. Furthermore, stability paths from the experiential variables at Year 1 to those at Year 3 were also hypothesized.

Method

Participants and Design

The sample consists of adolescents from three cohorts of the Sloan Study for Youth and Social Development (Csikszentmihalyi & Schneider, 2000). Initial data collection occurred when participants were students in Grades 6, 8, and 10, and a second wave of data was collected 2 years later. The participants came from 12 sites across the United States that were selected to represent urban, suburban, and rural community contexts with a wide range of socioeconomic conditions. Within each site, adolescents were recruited for participation from one high school and one or two of its principal feeder elementary and middle schools. From an initial pool of 877 who, along with their parents, consented to participate, only those who completed at least 15 Experience Sampling Method (ESM) response forms (discussed later) in each wave and had complete questionnaire data were retained for analysis (N = 236). The rigorous selection criteria were necessary to ensure the validity of the ESM data as a representation of adolescents' daily lives, but the trade-off was a final sample with greater proportions of girls, Whites, Asians, and students with higher SES than in the initial pool. Boys made up 36.4% of the sample; 28.4% of the sample were 6th graders, 37.7% were 8th graders, and 33.9% were 10th graders; 72.0% of the sample were White, 11.4% were African American, 9.7% were Hispanic, and 6.8% were Asian. Approximately one third of the parents had a college degree, one third had less education, and one third had postgraduate education.

During each wave of data collection (Years 1 and 3), participants completed a questionnaire and a booklet of ESM response forms. The booklet was completed over the course of 1 week, with participants filling out a new form in response to each signal from a preprogrammed wristwatch. During the ESM week, the watch beeped at a random time during every 2-hr block from 7:30 a.m. to 10:30 p.m. daily. The response form included both open-ended and scaled items. Csikszentmihalyi and Larson (1987) provided a detailed description of this methodology and several indications of its validity and reliability. In the study reported here, participants completed an average of 35 response forms in Year 1 and 29 in Year 3, for a total of 15,147 responses from all participants over the 2 years.

Measures

Family context. The degree of support and challenge the adolescent perceived in the social environment of the family was measured by an adaptation of the Complex Family Questionnaire (CFQ), an instrument developed by Rathunde (1996) and Csikszentmihalyi et al. (1993). On the CFQ, each dimension is measured by 16 statements that participants indicated either applied or did not apply in their families. (A list of items in each scale is available from the author.) Support included items that focus on family cohesion and care for one another, such as "Others notice when I'm feeling down, even if I don't say anything." Challenge was tapped by items relating to encouragement of individuality and accomplishment, such as "I'm expected to do my best" and "It's important to be self-confident and independent and to earn respect." Internal consistencies, as measured by Cronbach's alpha, were acceptable: support, $\alpha = .81$; challenge, $\alpha = .72$.

School context. School support was measured by a series of six questionnaire items asking participants to rate their level of agreement with statements about teacher attitudes and practices toward students. One such item is, "When I work hard on schoolwork, my teachers praise my effort." For school challenge, four items were used in which participants rated how often they were asked to show they really understood the material in class, rather than asked to just give an answer. Each of the items pertained to a different academic subject area. (A list of items in each scale is available from the author.) Cronbach alphas for school support and school challenge were $\alpha = .75$ and $\alpha = .84$, respectively.

SES. Although family SES is commonly measured with data on parental income, occupation, and education, the first two of these types of data were not gathered due to reliance on adolescent self-report. The remaining indicator of family SES, parent education, was reported by the adolescent and was coded into three categories, corresponding to less than, equal to, or more than a 4-year college degree for the parent with the highest level of education. To supplement this measure, a measure of home resources was computed as the total number of resources adolescents reported from a list that included magazines, a computer, a daily newspaper, and reference and other books. These resources provide access to information and thereby may facilitate the growth of skills. Finally, a community-level social class variable was created based on neighborhood census tract data to categorize each of the sites included in the study according to the five levels ranging from 1 (*poor*) to 5 (*upper class*) of the Hollingshead (1975) Four-Factor Index. Although this variable may loosely indicate family SES, it is more valuable as an indicator of community resources and opportunities.

Experiential variables. Variables measured via the ESM included two activity measures (proportion of time engaged in productive activities and in active leisure) and four measures of cognitive and motivational aspects of experience while engaged in productive activities (autonomy, intrinsic motivation, concentration, and goal-directedness). Participants' responses to the open-ended question "What was the main thing you were doing as you were signaled?" were coded into several broad categories. The two of interest to this study are productive activities and active leisure. The former includes doing schoolwork whether in school or not, attending to a school class, and doing volunteer or paid work. Just being in school was not sufficient to qualify as a productive activity; participants had to indicate that a productive activity was the main thing they were doing at the moment. Active leisure includes doing extracurricular activities, playing sports or games, and doing artwork or hobbies. This coding scheme has been used in many previous ESM studies of adolescents (e.g., Adlai-Gail, 1994; Csikszentmihalyi et al., 1993) with good reliability. The percentage of an individual's responses within any category relative to his or her total number of responses for the week was taken as an indication of the proportion of time the person spent doing activities in that category.

Variables measuring the cognitive and motivational aspects of experience during productive activities were created from scaled or categorical ESM questions. Within each year, responses were aggregated across only those response forms on which the participant indicated engagement in productive activities. The participants' degree of autonomy during productive activities was assessed by an item asking them whether they were doing their current activity because they wanted to, had to, or had nothing else to do. The perception of free choice versus coercion or external pressure to act is inferred to indicate an autonomy-supportive social context. Thus, the percentage of productive-activity responses on which an individual expressed free choice ("wanting to" do the activity) was used as the measure of autonomy. Intrinsic motivation was assessed by three rating scales: interest, enjoyment, and wish to be doing something else (reversed). These three grouped on one factor in a factor analysis of ESM scales and showed acceptable in-

ternal consistency ($\alpha = .72$) as a composite measure of intrinsic motivation. Although intrinsic motivation, as expected, was significantly correlated with autonomy, $r = .31$, the two constructs have less than 10% of their variance in common and are considered to measure separate concepts. Goal-directedness was measured by one item on which participants rated how important their current activity was to their future goals. Strength of concentration was also assessed by one ESM item, "How well were you concentrating?"

Procedure

After a group orientation during which watches, ESM booklets, and questionnaires were distributed, all participants in a school completed the ESM during the same week. Participants were asked to keep the watch and the booklet with them whenever possible and to respond to as many signals as possible.

Results

Within-Time Structural Equation Models

Means, standard deviations, and correlations among the 15 variables included in the proposed structural equation models are presented in Table 1. Maximum likelihood estimation, based on the variance–covariance matrix and calculated by the Amos computer program (Arbuckle, 1997), was employed to estimate the parameters of all models. To assess the associations between specific contextual and individual variables and specific experiential variables, the first model did not include any latent constructs, as described earlier. A fully saturated model was estimated, and then the nonsignificant paths, as indicated by the Wald test, were fixed to zero and the model was reestimated, as recommended by Chou and Bentler (1990). The reduced model fit the data well, $\chi^2(65, N = 236) = 77.7, p = .14$, GFI = .96, CFI = .98, RMSEA = .029.[1] The remaining parameter estimates, shown in Table 2, did not differ appreciably from those in the saturated model. As in multiple regression analyses, these parameters estimate the effect of one variable on another while controlling for all other variables in the model. The estimates indicate that school challenge was positively related to goal-directedness, intrinsic motivation, and concentration, whereas school support and family support each had only one signifi-

---

[1] Acceptable fit was taken to be indicated by a nonsignificant chi-square (*p* value above .05), goodness-of-fit index (GFI) and Bentler's (1990) comparative fit index (CFI) above .90, and root mean square error of approximation (RMSEA) below .05 (Brown & Cudeck, 1993).

Table 1. *Correlations, Means, and Standard Deviations for All Variables Used in Models*

	1	2	3	4	5	6	7	8	9	10	11	12	13	14	15
1. Family Challenge	.54	.41	.17	.25	-.01	-.09	.10	.12	.19	.37	.07	.07	.15	.26	.08
2. Family Support	.70	.52	.14	.24	.00	-.18	.15	.04	.15	.25	.02	.10	.13	.22	.06
3. School Challenge	.30	.29	.26	.26	-.16	.06	.04	.07	-.01	.11	.10	.03	.10	.15	-.09
4. School Support	.32	.39	.22	.47	-.03	-.03	.03	.01	-.03	.08	.08	.16	.22	.28	.05
5. Autonomy	.03	.08	-.11	.10	.19	-.19	.02	-.13	-.16	-.07	.11	.14	.20	-.01	-.11
6. Grade	-.09	-.18	.06	-.03	.19	1.0	.06	.02	-.04	.04	.13	.13	-.06	.09	-.04
7. Male	.10	.15	.04	.03	-.19	.06	1.0	.02	.12	.09	-.06	.02	-.11	.03	.18
8. Community SES	.12	.04	.07	.01	-.13	.05	.02	1.0	.49	.38	-.14	-.12	-.05	.16	.23
9. Parent Education	.19	.15	-.01	-.03	-.16	-.04	.12	.49	1.0	.59	-.07	-.08	-.07	.13	.18
10. Home Resources	.37	.25	.11	.08	-.07	.04	.09	.38	.59	1.0	-.03	-.07	.04	.19	.18
11. Goal Directed	.26	.24	.23	.22	.09	.07	-.03	-.23	-.09	-.02	.44	.22	.26	.10	-.02
12. Intrinsic Motivation	.22	.30	.21	.32	.31	-.14	.01	-.17	-.11	-.08	.33	.40	.25	.19	-.04
13. Concentration	.32	.32	.24	.24	.04	-.10	-.01	-.19	-.09	.02	.41	.43	.47	.12	.01
14. Productive	.19	.10	.01	.09	-.06	.28	.23	-.11	-.06	-.04	.20	.10	.17	.27	-.03
15. Active Leisure	.18	.21	.13	.12	.03	-.28	.27	.23	.25	.20	-.04	.00	-.06	-.15	.26
Year 1															
M	10.9	11.1	2.31	4.35	13.7	8.11	0.36	3.47	2.03	5.59	5.25	4.46	7.17	26.3	14.1
SD	3.1	3.9	1.2	1.8	18.7	1.6	0.48	1.1	0.80	1.5	2.1	1.4	1.5	10.5	9.5
Year 3															
M	11.0	10.2	2.74	4.45	10.7	10.1	0.36	3.47	2.03	5.59	5.26	4.57	7.21	33.4	9.89
SD	3.2	3.9	1.0	1.7	13.3	1.6	0.48	1.1	0.80	1.5	1.9	1.3	1.5	13.2	7.5

Note: $N = 236$. For $.13 \leq r \leq .17$, $p < .05$. For $.18 \leq r \leq .22$, $p < .01$. For $r \geq .23$, $p < .001$. Correlations between Year 1 variables (in rows) and Year 3 variables (columns) appear on the diagonal and below the diagonal. Correlations within Year 1 appear above the diagonal. SES = socioeconomic status.

Table 2. *Standardized Parameter Estimates From Year 1 Model With No Latent Constructs*

	Goal Directed	Intrinsic Motivation	Concentration	Productive Activities	Active Leisure
Family Challenge	.24	—	.28	.23	—
Family Support	—	.15	—	—	—
School Challenge	.16	.18	.17	—	—
School Support	—	.16	—	—	—
Autonomy	—	.28	—	—	—
Grade	.12	—	—	.29	−.30
Parent Education	—	—	—	—	—
Community SES	−.27	−.15	−.23	−.16	.24
Home Resources	—	—	—	—	—
Male	—	—	—	.19	.28

Note: $N = 236$. All parameters significant, $p < .05$. SES = socioeconomic status.

cant path to intrinsic motivation. Family challenge had significant paths to productive activities, goal-directedness, and concentration. Independent of these effects, intrinsic motivation was also predicted by autonomy. Of the SES variables, only social class of community retained significant paths, whereby residing in a more affluent community was associated with more time spent in active leisure and less time in productive activities. In addition, community social class had negative paths to goal-directedness, intrinsic motivation, and concentration. Gender was associated with choice of activities, with adolescent boys doing more productive and active leisure activities. Finally, productive activities and the future importance (goal-directedness) of those activities increased with grade, whereas active leisure decreased with grade.

In the second within-time model, two latent constructs were created to represent the proposed global measures of context and experience. Support and challenge in the school and family contexts were hypothesized to indicate the latent construct of growth-conducive environment. Goal-directedness, intrinsic motivation, and concentration during productive activities were conceptualized as indicators of growth-conducive experiences. A third latent construct combining the three SES variables was considered but rejected on the basis of the lack of significant paths from parent education and home resources. As such, the latter two variables were dropped from the model and community social class was retained as a stand-alone indicator of SES.

The model, illustrated in its final form in Figure 1, was estimated in three steps. In the first step, the latent factor measurement paths and all of the standard structural pathways were estimated. Then, as earlier, the Wald test was used to determine which paths to eliminate to improve the model fit. The remaining pathways resulting from this second step are represented in Figure 1 by all of the solid pathways. This model confirmed the validity of the two latent constructs, as signified by the significant and relatively large loadings, and it also resulted in several significant structural paths. However,

the fit of the model to the data was only marginal, $\chi^2(54, N = 236) = 93.1, p = .001$, GFI = .94, CFI = .93, RMSEA = .055.

Thus, modification indexes were examined to determine if model fit would improve by the freeing of any previously constrained parameters (Chou & Bentler, 1990). The indexes indicated that the addition of three nonstandard paths (paths to or from specific indicators of latent constructs) would significantly improve model fit.[2] The three paths, from school support and autonomy to intrinsic motivation and from grade to goal-directedness, were consistent with theory and allowed the model to examine both global and specific predictive pathways simultaneously.

In the third step, the addition of these nonstandard paths (represented in the figure by dashed lines) resulted in a significant improvement in model fit, with the final model fitting the data well, $\chi^2(51, N = 236) = 58.7, p = .22$, GFI = .97, CFI = .99, RMSEA = .025. The final model illustrates that global growth-conducive environment significantly predicted growth-conducive experience and the proportion of time spent engaging in productive activities and active leisure. In addition, school support and autonomy each had an additional unique effect on motivation. Community social class was negatively associated with growth-conducive experience. The other structural paths in the model were similar to those in the original model.

Across-Time Model

To assess the direct and indirect associations of the contextual, individual, and experiential variables across time, the third model extended the second by including the contextual, individual, and experiential variables

---

[2]Standard paths are from either a latent construct or a stand-alone measured variable to another latent construct or stand-alone measured variable. Limiting structural equation models to include only standard paths may omit important pathways (Hull, Tedlie, & Lehn, 1995; Newcomb, 1994).

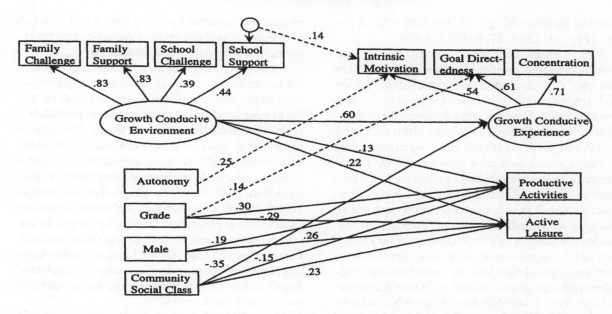

Figure 1. Within-year model with standardized parameter estimates for standard and nonstandard paths. For all parameters, *p* < .05. Solid lines denote standard pathway. Dotted lines denote nonstandard pathway.

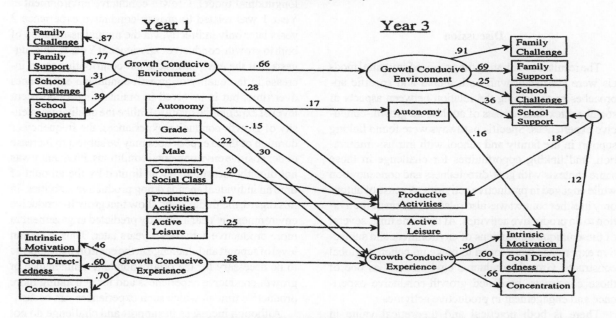

Figure 2. Final longitudinal model with standardized parameter estimates. For all parameters shown, *p* < .05. Structural paths within Year 1 were included in the model, but are not shown here. These paths are identical to those in Figure 1, with similar estimates.

from Year 3. Paths were included that represented both within-time and across-time hypothesized relations between the contextual and individual and experiential variables. In addition, stability paths were included between each Year 1 variable and the same variable at Year 3. As with the within-time models, a three-step approach was taken to estimate the model. The final model appears in Figure 2, although for clarity, the structural paths within Year 1 are not shown.

In the first step, all latent construct measurement paths and all of the standard structural pathways within and across time were estimated, with the exception that paths from Year 1 experiential variables to Year 3 con-

textual variables were constrained to zero.[3] Next, nonsignificant paths were constrained to zero in the second step, and the model was reestimated. Finally, nonstandard paths consistent with theoretical expectations and modification indexes were added. The final

---

[3] Although Year 1 experiential variables are positively correlated with Year 3 contextual variables, a direct causal relation (experience causing context) was not hypothesized. Rather, the relation was thought to be indirect, with both caused by either prior context or the (unmeasured) perceptual characteristics of the individual, or a combination of both.

model fit the data well, $\chi^2(203, N = 200) = 235.2, p = .06$, GFI = .91, CFI = .97, RMSEA = .028.

Both growth-conducive environment and growth-conducive experience showed strong stability over time. Growth-conducive environment did not directly predict growth-conducive experience across time or within Year 3. However, growth-conducive environment in Year 1 did have an indirect effect on Year 3 growth-conducive experience via its significant effect on Year 1 growth-conducive experience. Year 1 environment also had a direct positive effect on Year 3 productive activities. Autonomy in Year 1 had a direct effect on Year 3 growth-conducive experience and an additional unique indirect effect on Year 3 intrinsic motivation, via its effect on Year 3 autonomy. Year 1 autonomy was also negatively related to Year 3 active leisure. Community social class had only one significant longitudinal path to productive activities. Gender did not predict any Year 3 variable. Finally, growth-conducive experiences in Year 3 were also predicted by grade, meaning that such experiences increased with age.

Discussion

The results of estimating the proposed structural models were consistent with both global and specific approaches to explaining the relation between aspects of social context and aspects of adolescent growth-conducive experiences. Specific pathways were found linking support in the family and school with intrinsic motivation, and linking opportunities for challenge in those same contexts with goal-directedness and concentration while engaged in productive activities. A sense of autonomy in either context was also related to intrinsic motivation to do productive activities. At the same time, several of these unique dimensions of environment and subjective experience were found to make up coherent global constructs. Growth-conducive environment, as one of those constructs, predicted growth-conducive experience and engagement in productive activities.

There is both practical and theoretical value in maintaining and building on both types of models. The developmental-contextual approach emphasizes the interrelations among specific elements of changing contexts and characteristics of developing individuals (Lerner, 1998). To some extent, the sophistication of a developmental model could be judged by the degree of multidimensionality and differentiation with which both contexts and individuals are specified. Thus, in this study, knowing the specific relations between support and challenge in specific contexts and each of several dimensions of individual cognitive and affective experience is a first step toward developing even more sophisticated models involving more dimensions and more precisely specified dimensions of both context and individual experience. Such models would serve

parents and educators by giving them a tool by which to design and evaluate optimal growth-conducive environments for children and adolescents.

On the other hand, specific contextual and experiential factors do not operate in isolation. The synthesis of these factors into more global constructs allows the testing of macrolevel relations that would not be evident in more differentiated models. For example, although none of the four indicators of growth-conducive environment predicted time spent in active leisure activities, the global construct did have a significant pathway linking it to active leisure. Furthermore, the strength of the link between growth-conducive environment and growth-conducive experience was greater than the strength of any of the specific pathways among the indicators of those constructs. Clearly, the confluence of several optimal environmental characteristics brings with it a greater developmental benefit than would be derived from the simple addition of each isolated characteristic.

The stability of environmental and experiential dimensions over 2 years was shown to be quite strong in the longitudinal model. Growth-conducive environment at Year 1 was related to growth-conducive experience 2 years later only indirectly, via the mutual association of both to growth-conducive experience at Year 1. This suggests that the environment is not contributing to an increase in the quality of growth-conducive experiences over time, but is involved in maintaining a consistent level of experiential quality. Unlike the qualitative intensity of growth-conducive experiences, the frequency or duration of these experiences may be subject to increase under positive environmental conditions. Frequency was not directly measured, but is limited by the amount of time an individual spends doing productive activities. In this regard, the findings did show that growth-conducive environment in Year 1 directly predicted engagement in more productive activities 2 years later. Thus, a certain level of support and challenge in the environment appears to be necessary for the origination and maintenance of growth-conducive experiences and for generating more productive time in which such experiences can occur.

Although increases in support and challenge do not increase the intensity of growth-conducive experiences over time, families and schools that facilitate autonomy do seem to be able to improve the quality of adolescents' experiences. Although there was no direct link between autonomy and growth-conducive experience within Year 1, there was a longitudinal link. In other words, an autonomy-supportive context appears to set the stage for future growth-conducive experience, probably by increasing intrinsic motivation in productive activities.

These results are consistent with results from a number of other studies. For example, Ginsburg and Bronstein (1993) and Grolnick and Ryan (1989) reported that autonomy-supportive family styles were associated with the intrinsic motivation and academic performance of preadolescents. Parents who praised their children's efforts and ability and encouraged independent problem solving had children who preferred more challenging tasks. Similar results have been obtained in school settings (e.g., Matthews, 1991). Roeser, Eccles, and Sameroff (1998) reported that a perceived school environment with positive interpersonal relations and support for competence and autonomy predicted eighth graders' motivation and achievement. The link between intrinsic motivation and opportunities for challenge appears to be reciprocal. Level of challenge offered in school, as indicated by high expectations and an emphasis on persistence and mastery, predicts intrinsic motivation (Gottfried, Fleming, & Gottfried, 1994; Mitchell, 1996). At the same time, intrinsic motivation can spur students to take more challenging courses (Wong & Csikszentmihalyi, 1991).

An alternative explanation for the links found between context and experience in this study (as well as in several previous studies) lies in the fact that the contextual factors measured here are to some degree determined by the individual's perception of them. Support and challenge in the school and family contexts and autonomy were all measured via the adolescent's self-report. Thus, these variables are not purely contextual or individual factors, but rather a combination of both. Perceptions of normal individuals are grounded in objective conditions, but individuals in the same objective environment can have widely varying perceptions. Thus, the links found here among the self-reported contextual dimensions and the experiential dimensions may reflect, to some degree, the consistency of adolescents in perceiving their environment and experiences along similar lines. This possibility leads to the conclusion that environmental conditions earlier in development interacted with innate individual characteristics to result in a consistent tendency to perceive things a certain way.

The one contextual dimension that was not measured using self-report, community social class, showed a negative concurrent relation with growth-conducive experience and productive activities but a positive association with active leisure. The negative association of SES with growth-conducive experience is puzzling; it may reflect the higher expectations of upper class adolescents (who rate their experiences lower, relative to their expectations) or a tendency of lower class adolescents to favor extreme responses. Two years later, this relation disappeared and community social class was positively related to productive activities. The change of direction of the relation between social class and productive activities may reflect different developmental trajectories among members of different social classes. In the period from 6th to 10th grade, adolescents from lower class communities are probably more likely to spend part of their time working for pay outside of school time (Entwisle, Alexander, Olson, & Ross, 1999), whereas those in more affluent communities have more time and opportunities to pursue sports and hobbies after school. As adolescents move into the later years of high school, the academic expectations and homework load placed on them (and their corresponding investment of time in these productive activities) may be greater in upper class communities than in lower class communities.

There was also an overall increase in productive activities with grade, as indicated in the within-year model. The developmental trajectory suggested by the results is one of increasing work, decreasing play (active leisure), and increasing goal-directedness. The trends for productive activities and active leisure can also be seen in the changes in means over 2 years (Table 1), consistent with theoretical expectations. Like autonomy, grade was also associated longitudinally but not concurrently with growth-conducive experiences. The lack of a cross-sectional effect, coupled with the positive longitudinal effect, suggests that little change takes place from 6th through 10th grade (assuming the cross-sectional result indicates developmental and not cohort effects) but that significant increases in growth-conducive experiences occur from 10th to 12th grade.

Such an increase may be due to the increase in challenge that adolescents perceive over time in their schools. Means presented here (Table 1) and previous analyses of these data (Hektner, 1996) showed that school challenge increased over the 2-year period. At the same time, school support and family challenge remained stable. Family support decreased over time, reflecting the normal developmental process of separation and differentiation from the family. Although this process would seem to require adolescents to take on an ever greater degree of autonomy over their activities, their autonomy during productive activities actually decreased over time. Thus, although they are being presented with greater challenges as they progress through school, they increasingly see engagement in those challenges as a requirement instead of a personal choice.

Further specification of the developmental trajectory of both contexts and experience should be a goal of future research. This study was limited to only two time points; the addition of several more points of measurement would allow the use of growth-curve analysis to detect nonlinear trajectories and individual differences in growth. A further refinement and extension of this study would employ both self-reported and more objective measures of growth-conducive environment. This would enable a more precise model of the interaction between context and individual in the process of development.

Despite these limitations, this study extended previous work along several dimensions. First, it is based on a diverse, national sample of adolescents. Second, the data on time allocation in various activities and subjective experience during engagement in those activities were derived by sampling experience on multiple occasions during each wave of data collection. This method combines the ecological validity of naturalistic observation with the precision of scaled questionnaire measures. Finally, the use of structural equation modeling allowed the testing of both global and specific developmental pathways both within and across time.

The findings from this study have both practical and theoretical relevance. Csikszentmihalyi et al. (1993) concluded that in adolescence, "a talent will be developed if it produces optimal experiences" (p. 252). If parents and educators are to facilitate the development of talent of the adolescents in their care, they will need to find ways of creating environments conducive to optimal experiences. As these data show, such environments would offer interpersonal support, autonomy, and opportunities to pursue challenges related to future goals. Although schools are structured to provide increasing levels of challenge as students develop, this structure may not be as well adapted to provide students with greater levels of autonomy over their productive time and with a consistent level of interpersonal support. Educational and community policies that take into account all three of these goals should prove to be the most effective at promoting the optimal development of all adolescents.

References

Adlai-Gail, W. S. (1994). *Exploring the autotelic personality.* Unpublished doctoral dissertation, University of Chicago.

Arbuckle, J. L. (1997). *AMOS user's guide, version 3.6.* Chicago: SmallWaters.

Bentler, P. (1990). Comparative fit indexes in structural models. *Psychological Bulletin, 107,* 238–246.

Bronfenbrenner, U. (1979). *The ecology of human development: Experiments by nature and design.* Cambridge, MA: Harvard University Press.

Brown, M. W., & Cudeck, R. (1993). Alternative ways of assessing model fit. In K. A. Bollen & J. S. Long (Eds.), *Testing structural equation models* (pp. 136–162). Newbury Park, CA: Sage.

Chou, C.-P., & Bentler, P. M. (1990). Model modification in covariance structure modeling: A comparison among likelihood ratio, Lagrange multiplier, and Wald tests. *Multivariate Behavioral Research, 25,* 115–136.

Csikszentmihalyi, M. (1988). The flow experience and its significance for human psychology. In M. Csikszentmihalyi & I. S. Csikszentmihalyi (Eds.), *Optimal experience: Psychological studies of flow in consciousness* (pp. 15–35). New York: Cambridge University Press.

Csikszentmihalyi, M. (1990). *Flow: The psychology of optimal experience.* New York: Harper & Row.

Csikszentmihalyi, M., & Larson, R. (1984). *Being adolescent: Conflict and growth in the teenage years.* New York: Basic Books.

Csikszentmihalyi, M., & Larson, R. (1987). Validity and reliability of the experience sampling method. *Journal of Nervous and Mental Disease, 175,* 526–536.

Csikszentmihalyi, M., Rathunde, K., & Whalen, S. (1993). *Talented teenagers: The roots of success and failure.* New York: Cambridge University Press.

Csikszentmihalyi, M., & Schneider, B. (2000). *Becoming adult: How teenagers prepare for work.* New York: Basic Books.

Deci, E. L. (1992). The relation of interest to the motivation of behavior: A self-determination theory perspective. In K. A. Renninger, S. Hidi, & A. Krapp (Eds.), *The role of interest in learning and development* (pp. 43–70). Hillsdale, NJ: Lawrence Erlbaum Associates, Inc.

Deci, E. L. (1995). *Why we do what we do: The dynamics of personal autonomy.* New York: Putnam.

Deci, E. L., & Ryan, R. M. (1985). *Intrinsic motivation and self-determination in human behavior.* New York: Plenum.

Deci, E. L., & Ryan, R. M. (1987). The support of autonomy and the control of behavior. *Journal of Personality and Social Psychology, 53,* 1024–1037.

Entwisle, D. R., Alexander, K. L., Olson, L. S., & Ross, K. (1999). Paid work in early adolescence: Developmental and ethnic patterns. *Journal of Early Adolescence, 19,* 363–388.

Ford, D. H., & Lerner, R. M. (1992). *Developmental systems theory: An integrative approach.* Newbury Park, CA: Sage.

Ginsburg, G. S., & Bronstein, P. (1993). Family factors related to children's intrinsic/extrinsic motivational orientation and academic performance. *Child Development, 64,* 1461–1474.

Gottfried, A. E. (1991). Maternal employment in the family setting: Developmental and environmental issues. In J. V. Lerner & N. L. Galambos (Eds.), *Employed mothers and their children* (pp. 63–84). New York: Garland.

Gottfried, A. E., Fleming, J. S., & Gottfried, A. W. (1994). Role of parental motivational practices in children's academic intrinsic motivation and achievement. *Journal of Educational Psychology, 86,* 104–113.

Gottfried, A. E., Fleming, J. S., & Gottfried, A. W. (1998). Role of cognitively stimulating home environment in children's academic intrinsic motivation: A longitudinal study. *Child Development, 69,* 1448–1460.

Grolnick, W. S., & Ryan, R. M. (1989). Parent styles associated with children's self-regulation and competence in school. *Journal of Educational Psychology, 81,* 143–154.

Hektner, J. M. (1996). *Exploring optimal personality development: A longitudinal study of adolescents.* Unpublished doctoral dissertation, University of Chicago.

Hektner, J. M. (1997, March). *Support and challenge: Encouraging the development of flow and intrinsic motivation in school.* Paper presented at the annual meeting of the American Educational Research Association, Chicago.

Hektner, J. M., & Csikszentmihalyi, M. (1996, April). A longitudinal exploration of flow and intrinsic motivation in adolescents. In U. Schiefele & D. Hickey (Chairs), *Experience sampling and on-line assessment of affect, motivation, and cognition in diverse learning contexts.* Symposium conducted at the annual meeting of the American Educational Research Association, New York.

Hollingshead, A. G. (1975). *Four factor index of social status.* Unpublished manuscript, Yale University, New Haven, CT.

Hull, J. G., Tedlie, J. C., & Lehn, D. A. (1995). Modeling the relation of personality variables to symptom complaints: The unique role of negative affectivity. In R. H. Hoyle (Ed.), *Structural equation modeling: Concepts, issues and applications* (pp. 217–235). Thousand Oaks, CA: Sage.

Lamborn, S., Mounts, N., Steinberg, L., & Dornbusch, S. (1991). Patterns of competence and adjustment among adolescents from authoritative, indulgent, and neglectful families. *Child Development, 62,* 1049–1065.

Lerner, R. M. (1998). Theories of human development: Contemporary perspectives. In W. Damon (Series Ed.) & R. M. Lerner (Vol. Ed.), *Handbook of child psychology: Vol. 1. Theoretical models of human development* (5th ed., pp. 1–24). New York: Wiley.

Matthews, D. B. (1991). The effects of school environment on intrinsic motivation of middle-school children. *Journal of Humanistic Education and Development, 30,* 30–36.

Mitchell, S. A. (1996). Relationships between perceived learning environment and intrinsic motivation in middle school physical education. *Journal of Teaching in Physical Education, 15,* 369–383.

Newcomb, M. D. (1994). Drug use and intimate relationships among women and men: Separating specific from general effects in prospective data using structural equation models. *Journal of Consulting and Clinical Psychology, 62,* 463–476.

Noom, M., & Dekovic, M. (1998). Family interaction as a context for the development of adolescent autonomy. In M. Hofer, J. Youniss, & P. Noack (Eds.), *Advances in applied developmental psychology: Vol. 15. Verbal interaction and development in families with adolescents* (pp. 109–125). Stamford, CT: Ablex.

Rathunde, K. (1996). Family context and talented adolescents' optimal experience in school-related activities. *Journal of Research on Adolescence, 6,* 605–628.

Roeser, R. W., Eccles, J. S., & Sameroff, A. J. (1998). Academic and emotional functioning in early adolescence: Longitudinal relations, patterns, and prediction by experience in middle school. *Development and Psychopathology, 10,* 321–352.

Silverberg, S. B., & Gondoli, D. M. (1996). Autonomy in adolescence: A contextual perspective. In G. R. Adams, R. Montemayor, & T. P. Gullotta (Eds.), *Advances in adolescent development: Vol. 8. Psychosocial development during adolescence* (pp. 12–61). Thousand Oaks, CA: Sage.

Steinberg, L., Lamborn, S., Dornbusch, S., & Darling, N. (1992). Impact of parenting practices on adolescent achievement: Authoritative parenting, school involvement, and encouragement to succeed. *Child Development, 63,* 1266–1281.

Wong, M. M. (1993). *Autonomy, quality of experience, and academic performance.* Unpublished doctoral dissertation, University of Chicago.

Wong, M. M., & Csikszentmihalyi, M. (1991). Motivation and academic achievement: The effects of personality traits and the quality of experience. *Journal of Personality, 59,* 539–574.

Received December 13, 1999
Final revision received July 5, 2000
Accepted August 23, 2000

Applied Developmental Science
2001, Vol. 5, No. 3, 184–194

Family Socialization Practices and Their Effects on the Internalization of Educational Values for Asian and White American Adolescents

Kiyoshi Asakawa
Shikoku Gakuin University, Japan

Based on the theories of internalization and the self, this article examines effective family socialization practices of Asian and White Americans. The results indicated that parental support for autonomy and adolescents' perceived competence while studying favorably affected Asian Americans' internalization of their cultural values relevant to education and academic success. In contrast, for White Americans, these internalization factors did not have a substantial effect on adolescents' school performance. Moreover, for Asian Americans, parents' attitudes had stronger effects on adolescents' school performance in comparison to White American adolescents, whose teacher-awarded grades were attributed to their own academic aspirations. Differences in family socialization practices between Asian and White Americans are discussed within a context of underlying cultural frameworks that promote adolescents' school performance.

The popular literature through the 1980s and 1990s placed considerable attention on the academic success of Asian American students. This public attention was part of a much wider discussion of Asian Americans' success as a minority group in the United States beginning as early as the mid-1960s, when the term *model minority* was coined for this population. Some researchers, however, have claimed that this Asian American image of success is largely a myth produced by empirical analyses that miss important dimensions of socioeconomic indicators (Hirschman & Wong, 1984, 1986; Hurh & Kim, 1989; Suzuki, 1977; Takaki, 1989; Wong & Hirschman, 1983). Hurh and Kim (1989), for example, pointed out, "the common measurement of the Asian Americans' 'success' which does not test the investment aspect of Asian Americans' socio-economic status is conceptually too simplistic and thus distorts the complex reality of Asian Americans' labor market experiences" (p. 527). According to the researchers, Asian Americans pay a higher price than Whites for achieving a given level of educational attainment, such as working longer hours, including the time spent over weekends (see also Hirschman & Wong, 1984, 1986; Suzuki, 1977; Takaki, 1989; Wong & Hirschman, 1983).

Although the relative income advantages of educational performance for Asian Americans have been questioned, the high academic attainment of this population has been largely recognized as a reality based on

empirical evidence, such as Asian Americans' high grades and consistently high scores on college entrance exams (College Board, 1989). Several possible explanations have been suggested to explain these results. Although some of the explanations emphasize genetic factors (Herrnstein & Murray, 1994; Jensen & Inouya, 1980; Lynn & Dziobon, 1980), a familiar and more widely accepted explanation assumes that Asian cultural values and practices promote academic excellence (Kitano, 1984; Sue & Okazaki, 1990; Vernon, 1982). For example, using structured interviews with Harvard undergraduates and secondary summer school students of Asian ethnicity, Mordkowitz and Ginsburg (1987) reported that emphasis on academic study as the child's principal obligation, high parental expectations for achievement, parental control of after-school time, and prioritization of education in the family were pervasive themes. Using in-depth interviews with Japanese American parents and their children, Schneider, Hieshima, Lee, and Plank (1992) also suggested the indirect value of socialization processes in the family as key to Japanese Americans' educational success.

Incongruent findings of cross-cultural studies on family socialization suggest that there are different ways of parenting that effectively promote academic development of children from different cultures (Chao, 1994; Dornbusch, Ritter, Leiderman, Roberts, & Fraleigh, 1987; Steinberg, Dornbusch, & Brown, 1992). Dornbusch et al. (1987) investigated the relation between Baumrind's (1971) parenting styles and academic achievement among diverse ethnic groups and found that within ethnic groups, the authoritarian style and the permissive style were negatively related to academic grades, whereas the authoritative style

---

I thank all the Sloan Project members for their help in organizing the study and collecting and coding the data.

Requests for reprints should be sent to Kiyoshi Asakawa, Department of Education, Shikoku Gakuin University, 3-2-1 Bunkyo-cho, Zentsuji, Kagawa 765–8505, Japan. E-mail: asak@sg-u.ac.jp

was positively related. However, the researchers also found that Asian American students had the highest grades among all groups, including African Americans, Hispanics, White, and others; yet they came from families characterized as more authoritarian and permissive and less authoritative. Thus, although Baumrind's parenting styles explained achievement levels within ethnic groups, they failed to account for between-group differences.

Commenting on these results, Chao (1994) pointed out that Baumrind's (1971) parenting styles are not adequate to interpret the difference in academic performance between Asians and Whites "because Baumrind's conceptualizations are specific only to European-American culture" (p. 1113). According to Chao, the concept of authoritarian describes the optimal Chinese parenting style, but it does not capture the important features of caring for and loving that underlie Chinese parenting practices. It is not yet clear what the optimal parenting style is for Asian Americans. The theoretical arguments on parenting styles of culturally different groups suggest that there may be diverse mechanisms in the communication between parents and children from different cultures that promote high academic performance.

Additional studies have attempted to incorporate sociological and historical factors into their explanations of ethnic differences in academic performance (Alva, 1993; Hirschman & Wong, 1986; Ogbu, 1983, 1987, 1991; Sue & Kitano, 1973; Sue & Okazaki, 1990; Suzuki, 1977). For example, Ogbu has classified minorities into two categories, voluntary and involuntary, defining the former as immigrants who voluntarily came to the United States in search of a better life (e.g., Asian Americans) and the latter as immigrants who were incorporated into the United States through slavery or conquest (e.g., African Americans, Mexicans, Hawaiians). According to Ogbu (1987), differences in academic attainment between voluntary and involuntary immigrants are due to their perceptions regarding future opportunities, which in turn influence their perceptions of and responses to schooling. Asian Americans as a voluntary minority tend to do well in school because they understand schooling as a necessary step to social mobility. Sue and Okazaki (1990) argued that the academic success of Asian Americans is "a product of cultural values (i.e., ethnicity) and status in society (minority group standing)" (p. 917). Asians' perceived limitations in mobility in noneducational types of endeavors increase the relative value or function of education as a means of achieving success in a society where they have experienced occupational discrimination (for a similar argument, see also Schneider et al., 1992; Schneider & Lee, 1990).

More recently, using the Experience Sampling Method (ESM), Asakawa and Csikszentmihalyi (1998a, 1998b, 2000) examined the phenomenology of Asian and White American adolescents' everyday life experiences and suggested that the internalization of cultural values relevant to academic attainment may be a significant reason for the high academic achievement of Asian Americans. Asakawa and Csikszentmihalyi (1998b) further examined how parental practices differ between Asian and White American groups in terms of academic concerns and found that Asian American parents were more likely to organize and structure their children's lives for academic success, but less likely to get overly involved in their children's actual academic activities than their White American counterparts. These parental attitudes were also reported by Shoho (1994) for Japanese Americans in Hawaii during the 1930s and 1940s.

Theories of internalization (Deci & Ryan, 1985; Grusec & Goodnow, 1994) provide a new perspective for looking at the parenting practices of Asian Americans. These theories suggest that for internalization to occur, the socializing agents must provide children with support for autonomy as well as clear structure or guidelines. Thus, Asian American parenting practices reported by Asakawa and Csikszentmihalyi (1998b) and Shoho (1994) appear to be conducive to enhancing the internalization of values relevant to education and academic success. Ryan and his associates (Deci & Ryan, 1985; Ryan, Connell, & Grolnick, 1992; Ryan & Powelson, 1991) have proposed three basic psychological needs that promote the internalization process: autonomy, competence, and relatedness. If Asian Americans' academic success has something to do with internalization of values relevant to education, it is important to examine how these internalization factors affect the school performance of Asian and White American adolescents.

The Asian American sample examined in this study includes Chinese, Filipinos, Japanese, Koreans, Southeast Asians, and South Asians. We treated these diverse Asian groups under a single heading of Asian American based on the work of Markus and Kitayama (1991), who argued that in many Asian cultures, the self is viewed "not as separate from the social context but as more connected and less differentiated from others" (p. 227). This is in contrast to American culture, which has a different conception of the self that emphasizes independence from others by focusing on the individual and his or her unique inner attributes. Markus and Kitayama referred to the former view of the self as *interdependent* and the latter as *independent.* Moreover, they further pointed out that "the distinctions ... between independent and interdependent construals must be regarded as general tendencies that may emerge when the members of the culture are considered as a whole" (p. 225). Based on these theoretical assumptions, it is hypothesized that the Asian and White Americans in this study would be more likely to have interdependent and independent selves respectively, and their distinctive psychological tendencies would be reflected in both children's and parents' communication styles and attitudes toward academics.[1]

Drawing on the theories of internalization and the self, three major analyses were conducted. First, Asian and White American adolescents were compared with respect to their levels of perceived competence when engaged in academic activities, in activities perceived as more like work (i.e., worklike activities), and in activities thought to be important for their future goals. Previous studies have identified certain Asian family values, such as the importance of hard work, respect for education, and high expectations for achievement, as promoting Asian Americans' high educational attainment (Kitano, 1984; Mordkowitz & Ginsburg, 1987; Sue & Kitano, 1973; Sue & Okazaki, 1990; Vernon, 1982). If Asian American adolescents had internalized such values, their levels of perceived competence might be higher than those of White American adolescents when engaged in academic activities, worklike activities, and activities important to future goals.

Second, constructing two new variables, autonomy and structure, with the same parental practice items used in a previous study (Asakawa & Csikszentmihalyi, 1998b), this study examined how families from different backgrounds employed such practices (i.e., autonomy support and provision of structure). It was expected that academic socialization practices of Asian American families would differ from those employed by mainstream American families in promoting academic excellence.

Finally, this study explored whether parental autonomy support, provision of structure, and students' perceived competence in academic activities (the factors identified as promoting the process of internalization in Deci and Ryan's, 1985, theory), as well as student background characteristics and parents' and students' attitudes, would predict students' self-reported grades for both Asian and White American groups. If Asian American adolescents had internalized values related to the importance of education and academic success, and if internalization was a significant reason for their academic attainment, then the internalization factors (i.e., parental autonomy support, provision of structure, and students' perceived competence in actual academic activities) should predict Asian American students' school performance. An underlying hypothesis was that there may exist culturally diverse models of parental influence on children's academic development.

[1]Some studies (Ima & Rumbaut, 1989; Lee, 1994) have suggested that diversity may exist within this Asian American sample, and we certainly need to be cautious of problems associated with lumping together different Asian American groups. However, for the purpose of testing Markus and Kitayama's (1991) conceptions of self, we treat our Asian American sample as a single group.

Methods

Participants

A total of 1,109 students in the 6th, 8th, 10th, and 12th grades participated in a 5-year longitudinal study of career development (Csikszentmihalyi & Schneider, 2000), in which students were selected from 33 public schools across the United States. The schools were chosen to reflect the full range of socioeconomic environments, from affluent suburbs to low-income, socially segregated, urban neighborhoods. Students were, in turn, randomly chosen with the aim of obtaining representative samples of their respective schools in terms of gender, race, ethnicity, and scholastic ability. Of these students, 856 completed at least 15 ESM forms, the minimum required for inclusion in the database.

In this study, 34 Asian American students whose first language was not English (an Asian language) and 392 White American students whose first language was English were selected with the aim of obtaining two culturally different groups of adolescents.[2] Twenty-eight out of the 34 Asian American students reported that they spoke primarily English in their daily lives at the time of study. Although there was no instrument to measure their levels of acculturation or the length of time they had been in the United States, considering their first languages, these Asian students are presumably first and second generation. In addition, their first socialization phase in an Asian language may have exposed them to Asian culture to the extent that they preserved their cultural identities.

The characteristics of the Asian and White groups are shown in Table 1. In terms of gender and family composition, these two groups were similarly represented. However, Asian American adolescents were overrepresented in the 12th grade and underrepresented in the 6th grade, as compared to White American adolescents. Asian American adolescents were more likely to come from upper middle-class communities and less likely to come from working-class and upper class communities than their White American counterparts. Hence, age (grade) and

[2]Among the 856 students who completed at least 15 ESM forms, 53 students were Asian (6.2%), 459 were White (53.6%), and the other 344 were a mixture of African American, Hispanic, and Native American. Of the Asian subsample, Pacific Island, West Asian, and Middle Eastern students were excluded because of their cultural dissimilarity from other Asian groups. Of the Asian students, 34 who answered that their first language was not English were selected as an Asian sample. The Asian American students in this sample included 14 Chinese, 3 Filipinos, 2 Japanese, 5 Koreans, 7 Southeast Asians (Vietnamese, Laotian, Cambodian/Kampuchean, Thai), 2 South Asians (Asian Indian, Pakistani, Sri Lankan), and 1 student whose parents were Chinese and Vietnamese. Of the 459 White students, 392 who answered that their first language was English were selected as a White sample.

Table 1. *Characteristics of Asian and White Groups*

Variable	Asian[a]	White[b]	Chi-Square	p Value	df
Gender (%)					
Male	50	45	0.33	ns (.57)	1
Female	50	55			
Age (%)					
6th	12	26	11.50	p < .01	3
8th	21	27			
10th	26	29			
12th	41	18			
Family Composition (%)					
Both Mother and Father[c]	71	71	0.005	ns (.94)	1
Other	29	29			
Social Class of Community (%)[d]					
Lower Class	2.9	1.3	29.49	p < .001	4
Working Class	2.9	23.5			
Middle Class	20.6	30.9			
Upper Middle Class	67.6	25.8			
Upper Class	5.9	18.6			

[a]$n = 34$. [b]$n = 392$. [c]Families that consist of mothers and fathers who are not divorced, separated, or remarried. [d]Social class of community is an index of the census characteristics of the neighborhood in which adolescents live. This information was obtained from the 1990 census.

social class of community were controlled for when the two groups were compared using analysis of covariance regression techniques.

Procedure

Participants in the ESM wore wristwatches that were programmed to beep at random times during every 2-hr block from 7:30 a.m. to 10:30 p.m. daily, with the restriction that no two signals would be less than 30 min apart. Students were signaled eight times each day over 7 consecutive days and were instructed to fill out an ESM form each time they were signaled. Students also completed several surveys, including the Teenage Life Questionnaire (TLQ), a modification of instruments used on the National Education Longitudinal Study of 1988 to 1994.[3] The TLQ provides information about the student's ethnic or religious background, family composition, the educational background and occupation of the parents, family socioeconomic status, parent involvement, academic and social guidance, and family expectations for postsecondary schooling.

Measures

Measures for this study were selected from the ESM and the TLQ.

[3]In addition, each student met one-on-one with a team member for an in-depth interview that lasted approximately 40 min. This student interview was designed to elicit detailed information about students' educational and career goals. Questions regarding aspects of each student's family life, friendships, and future expectations were also asked in the interview.

Students' perceived competence (control of the situation). Perceived competence, one of the major factors in promoting internalization, was measured by the following question from the ESM: "Did you feel in control of the situation?" Responses for feeling in control of the situation were given on a 10-point rating scale ranging from 0 (*not at all*) to 9 (*very much*). These responses were standardized by individual mean score and were aggregated within each person to measure his or her perceived competence in various activities.

Students' perceptions of activities. To define worklike activities and activities highly important to future goals, two questions from the ESM were used. Students' perceptions of worklike activities were measured by inquiring if the main activity they were doing seemed more like work, more like play, like both, or like neither. Perceived importance of activities to future goals was measured by the question "How important was it [the main activity] in relation to your future goals?" Responses were given on a 9-point rating scale ranging from 1 (*not at all*) to 9 (*very much*) and standardized by individual mean score, and then classified in terms of whether importance to future goals was high or low (above or below the mean). High future importance included responses where a student's ratings of the importance of activities for future goals was higher than his or her weekly average (above 0 on the standardized score). Asakawa and Csikszentmihalyi (1998b) reported that both Asian American and White American adolescents had very similar perceptions of worklike, playlike, like both, and like neither activities, as well as activities important for their future goals.

Academic expectations of parents and adolescents. Parents' academic expectations and the student's own academic aspirations were measured by asking "How far in school do you think your father and your mother (or guardian) want you to go?" and "As things stand now, how far in school do you think you will get?" Answers for parents' expectations were coded for father's and mother's expectations separately, with four education categories: 1 (*less than high school graduation*), 2 (*graduate from high school*), 3 (*graduate from college*), and 4 (*attend a higher level of school after graduating from college*). The higher score of either the father's or mother's expectations was used as an index of the parents' educational expectations. The student's own academic aspirations were also coded using the same four categories.

Parental practices concerning academics. To measure parental practices concerning academics, three questions were included:

1. Who makes the decision was measured by the question "In your family, who makes most of the decisions on each of the following topics?" Two items relevant to this analysis were selected out of the seven original items. These are questions about who makes the decisions on what classes the student takes in school and on whether the student should go to college. Answers were given on 5-point scales (1 = *I decide by myself,* 2 = *I decide after discussing it with my parents,* 3 = *we decide together after discussing,* 4 = *my parents decide after discussing it with me,* 5 = *my parents decide themselves*).

2. Parental involvement in academic activities was measured by the question "How often do your parents do the following?" Six items ask how often, for instance, parents check on whether the student has done his or her homework or how often parents help the student with his or her homework. Answers were given on 4-point scales ranging from 0 (*never*) to 3 (*often*).

3. Frequency of discussion with parents was measured by the question "Since the beginning of the school year, how often have you discussed the following with either or both of your parents or guardians?" Selected items ask how often students have discussed, for instance, selecting courses or programs at school, things studied in class, or their grades. Answers were given on 3-point scales (1 = *not at all,* 2 = *once or twice,* 3 = *three or more times*).

Self-reported grades. Students' self-reported grades were measured by asking "Which of the following statements best describes your grades on your last report card?" Answers were given on an 8-point scale (1 = *mostly As,* 2 = *about half As and half Bs,* 3 = *mostly Bs,* 4 = *about half Bs and half Cs,* 5 = *mostly Cs,* 6 = *about half Cs and half Ds,* 7 = *mostly Ds,* 8 = *mostly below D*). These responses were recoded so that the higher the score, the better the grades students received on the report card.

Parental involvement in school activities. Students were asked, "In the first half of the school year, how often did either of your parents or guardians do any of the following?" Selected items ask how often parents or guardians attended school meetings, school events in which their children participated, and how often they volunteered at school. Answers were given on 3-point scales (1 = *never,* 2 = *once or twice,* 3 = *more than twice*).

Locus of control. Locus of control was measured by asking students to evaluate six statements on a 4-point scale (1 = *strongly disagree,* 2 = *disagree,* 3 = *agree,* 4 = *strongly agree*). Statements ranged from "I don't have enough control over the direction my life is taking" to "When I make plans, I am almost certain I can make them work." Answers were recoded so that the higher the score, the more students felt they had control.

Results

Adolescents' Perceived Competence in Ongoing Activities

Covariance analyses, controlling for the effects of age (grade) and social class of community, were performed to look for differences between Asian and White American adolescents in their levels of perceived competence when studying, when engaged in worklike activities, and when engaged in activities important to future goals.

Figure 1 shows the average z scores for both Asian American and White adolescents on their perceived competence in the three situations.[4] The results indicate that when they were engaged in studying, worklike activities, and activities important to their future goals, Asian American adolescents perceived themselves as more competent than White American adolescents; studying, $F(1, 416) = 6.05, p < .05$; worklike activities, $F(1, 416) = 10.17, p < .01$; activities important to future

---

[4]In computing z scores for each group, the weekly mean on a given item across all contexts and activities is set to zero. Average scores for a particular context that are above or below zero indicate deviation by each group from the mean for both groups for that week.

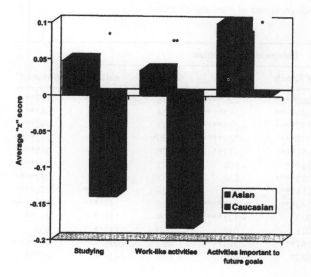

Figure 1. Asian American and White students' perceived competence in three situations. Comparison between groups: *$p <$ .05; **$p <$ .01; ***$p <$ .001.

goals, $F(1, 416) = 4.10$, $p < .05$.[5] Thus, Asian Americans' levels of perceived competence when studying, doing worklike activities, and doing activities important to their future goals appears to be more conducive to enhancing internalization of values of hard work, respect for education, and high expectations for achievement than those of White American adolescents.

Autonomy Support and Provision of Structure for Academic Success

Based on the findings of previous studies (Asakawa & Csikszentmihalyi, 1998b; Shoho, 1994), this study predicted that academic socialization practices of Asian American families would differ from those employed by mainstream American culture in promoting academic excellence. To examine this hypothesis, two new variables, autonomy and structure, were constructed using parental practice items that were examined separately in the previous study (Asakawa & Csikszentmihalyi, 1998b). First, these items were standardized because they were adopted originally from three different questions on the TLQ that used different rating scales. Then, the z scores for these items were used to construct the new variables. The autonomy variable was an average score derived from the following parental practice items: decision on what classes to take, check homework, help with homework, discussion about school courses, discussion about school activities, discussion about things studied, and discus-

[5]For this study, 426 students completed a total of 14,274 ESM forms (1,113 for the Asian sample and 13,161 for the White sample), which amounts to a response rate of about 60% (8 signals a day for 7 days × 426 students: 58% for Asians and 60% for Whites.

sion about grades. The higher the score, the more students had autonomy or freedom in actual academic activities. Structure was an average score based on the following parental practice items: decision on going to college, assign household chores, limit TV/game time, and discussion about standardized test plans and preparation. Again, the higher the score, the more parents provided their children with structure or guidance for academic success.

To determine how parental support for autonomy and provision of structure, as well as each parental practice item, were employed by families from different backgrounds, a set of multiple regression analyses were performed in which autonomy, structure, and each parental practice item were regressed on the background variables. Results are shown in Table 2.

Most of the regression coefficients for these parental practice items were significant for the variable Asian. This was not surprising given that the autonomy and structure variables were originally constructed based on Asian Americans' parental practices. However, for all autonomy items, family composition (intact family) and Asian origins appeared to yield different patterns. One might expect that adolescents from intact families would be more likely to succeed academically, as would Asian American adolescents, and that both intact families and Asian American families might therefore employ similar academic socialization practices. However, we found that Asian American parents were less likely to decide what classes their children should take ($p < .01$), helped their children with homework less often ($p < .001$), discussed school courses less often ($p < .05$), discussed school activities less often ($p < .05$), discussed things studied in class less often ($p < .01$), and discussed grades less often ($p < .001$) than White American parents. Parents from intact families were more likely to decide what classes their children should take ($p < .001$), checked whether their children had done their homework more often ($p < .001$), helped their children with homework more often ($p < .01$), discussed school courses more often ($p < .01$), discussed school activities more often ($p < .05$), discussed things studied in class more often ($p < .001$), and discussed grades more often ($p < .001$) than parents from nonintact families. These parental practices in intact families had totally different directions on the continuum of the level of autonomy support, as compared to those of Asian origins. If we use the concept of autonomy as constructed with Asian Americans' parental practices, we have to say that parents from intact families were less likely to support their children's autonomy in actual academic activities than their counterparts in nonintact families.

However, both parents from intact families and parents from Asian American families were more likely to structure their children's lives for academic success when compared to their counterparts. Parents from intact families were more likely to limit

Table 2. *Standardized Regression Coefficients From Multiple Regressions of Parental Practice Variables on Background Variables*

Dependent Variable	Independent Variables					Adjusted R^2
	SCC	Intact Family[a]	Grade	Gender[b]	Asian	
Autonomy[c]	−.049	−.260****	.220****	.038	.212****	.177****
Decision on What Classes to Take[d]	−.045	.166****	−.196****	.024	−.134***	.087****
Check Homework	−.067	.177****	−.375****	−.037	−.083*	.192****
Help With Homework	−.033	.179***	−.363****	.080*	−.158****	.212****
Discussion About School Courses[e]	.080*	.156***	.117**	.076	−.116**	.048****
Discussion About School Activities[e]	.169****	.118**	−.008	.025	−.120**	.048****
Discussion About Things Studied[e]	.089*	.212****	−.030	.037	−.153***	.072****
Discussion About Grades[e]	.035	.184****	−.003	−.026	−.212****	.071****
Structure[f]	.079*	.140***	−.251****	.049	.199****	.113****
Decision on Going to College[d]	.033	.033	−.131***	.004	.110**	.017**
Assign Household Chores	−.017	−.021	.018	−.010	−.125**	.005
Limit TV/Game Time	.064	.167****	−.301****	.007	.075	.120****
Discussion About SAT/ACT Plans and Preparations[e]	.064	.082*	−.028	.038	.121**	.017**

Note: SCC = social class of community.
[a]Intact family: Used as a dummy variable; where the family is intact, it equals 1, otherwise 0. [b]Gender: Used as a dummy variable; it equals 1 for boys and 2 for girls. [c]Autonomy: Average score of deciding on classes to take, checking homework, helping with homework, and discussions about school courses, about school activities, about things studied in school, and about grades. The higher the score, the more autonomy students have. [d]Decision making: The higher the score, the more parents make the decision. [e]Discussion: The higher the score, the more parents discuss with children. [f]Structure: Average score of deciding on going to college, assigning household chores, limiting TV time, and discussions about SAT/ACT plans and preparations. The higher the score, the more parents provide structure for academic success.
*$p < .10$. **$p < .05$. ***$p < .01$. ****$p < .001$.

TV/game time ($p < .001$) and to discuss plans and preparations for standardized tests ($p < .10$) than were parents from other types of families. Parents from Asian American families were also more likely to discuss plans and preparation for standardized tests with their children ($p < .05$) and were more likely to decide whether their children would attend college ($p < .05$). However, they were less likely to assign household chores to their children than White American parents. The academic socialization practices of Asian American parents were somewhat unique in providing support for their children's academic success compared to those that White American parents or parents from intact families were more likely to use. This point becomes much clearer if we directly examine the values for the constructed variables of autonomy and structure in Table 2.

Asian American parents were more likely to provide their children with freedom in actual academic activities than were White American parents ($p < .001$). On the other hand, parents from intact families were less likely to provide their children with freedom in their academic activities; that is, they were more likely to control their children's academic activities than parents from nonintact families ($p < .001$). It was found, however, that both parents from intact families and parents of Asian origin were more likely to provide their children with structure and guidance for academic success than their counterparts (intact family, $p < .01$; Asian, $p < .001$). Asian American parents appeared to use different socialization practices for their

children's academic success in comparison to White American parents as well as parents from intact families in general.

In addition, parents who had relatively older children were more likely to provide freedom in academic activities for their children and were less likely to provide structure for academic success than parents who had younger children (autonomy, $p < .001$; structure, $p < .001$).

Factors Promoting Students' School Performance

Two questions were examined. The first was whether internalization factors (i.e., parental autonomy support, provision of structure, and students' perceived competence while studying) would predict students' self-reported grades for both Asian American and White American groups. The second focused on whether factors such as background characteristics and several other variables concerning parents' and students' attitudes would predict students' school performance. Parental attitude variables include parents' educational expectations for their children; parental involvement in school activities such as attending school meetings, attending school events, and volunteering at school; provision of autonomy support; and provision of structure. Students' attitude variables include the student's own educational aspirations, locus of control, and perceived competence while studying. Regression analyses were performed for Asian and White American adolescents separately.

As shown in Table 3, Asian American parents' autonomy support and students' perceived competence predicted Asian American students' self-reported grades (autonomy, $p < .001$; competence, $p < .10$). However, none of the internalization factors directly predicted White American students' self-reported grades, although family structure (intact family) and gender had positive net effects on grades (intact family, $p < .10$; gender, $p < .10$). It appears that these internalization factors, especially parental autonomy support and students' perceived competence while studying, are fair predictors for the school performance of Asian Americans but not of White Americans.

When the relations between parents' and students' attitudes and students' school performance were examined, differential results were produced for Asian and White Americans. For White Americans, adolescents' own academic aspirations had positive net effects on their self-reported grades ($p < .001$). Locus of control was another strong predictor for White American adolescents' school performance ($p < .001$). For White American adolescents, their own attitudes, such as their educational aspirations and perceived locus of control, seemed to have strong positive effects on their school performance. In addi-

Table 3. *Standardized Regression Coefficients From Multiple Regressions of Adolescents' Self-Reported Grades on Background, Parent, and Student Variables*

Independent Variables	Asian Dependent Variables: Grades	White Dependent Variables: Grades
Background		
SCC	-.045	-.001
Intact Family[a]	.185	.088*
Grade (Age)	-.081	-.032
Gender[b]	-.052	.081*
Parent Variables		
Educational Expectations	.405**	-.076
Involvement in School Activities[c]	.550**	.133**
Provision of Autonomy[d]	.774****	.058
Provision of Structure[d]	.191	.060
Student Variables		
Educational Aspirations	.345**	.341****
Locus of Control[e]	.080	.156****
Perceived Competence[d]	.270**	.003
Adjusted R^2	.498***	.170****

Note: SCC = social class of community.
[a]Intact family: Used as a dummy variable, where intact family (mother and father) equals 1, otherwise equals 0. [b]Gender: Used as a dummy variable, where boys equal 1 and girls equal 2. [c]Involvement in school activities: attending school meetings, attending school events, and volunteering at school. [d]Internalization factors. [e]Locus of control: The higher the score, the more control students feel to have.
*$p < .10$. **$p < .05$. ***$p < .01$. ****$p < .001$.

tion, parental involvement in school activities had a positive net effect on White American adolescents' school grades ($p < .05$).

Asian American students' own educational aspirations and parental involvement in school activities had positive net effects on grades (educational aspirations, $p < .05$; parental involvement in school activities, $p < .05$), as observed for White Americans. However, two factors in parental attitudes (educational expectations and autonomy support), which were not significant predictors for White Americans' grades, had significant effects on Asian Americans' self-reported grades. If Asian American parents had higher educational expectations for their children and if they provided more freedom or autonomy support in actual academic activities, their children performed better in school (educational expectations, $p < .05$; autonomy support, $p < .001$).

Discussion

Previous studies by Asakawa and Csikszentmihalyi (1998a, 1998b, 2000) suggest that internalization of cultural values relevant to academic attainment and the importance placed on education may be significant reasons for the high academic achievement of Asian Americans. Ryan and his associates (Deci & Ryan, 1985; Ryan, 1991; Ryan et al., 1992; Ryan & Powelson, 1991) suggested that the process of internalization is promoted by three basic psychological needs for autonomy, competence, and relatedness. For internalization to occur, the socializing agents must provide children with support for autonomy as well as clear structure or guidance (Deci & Ryan, 1985; Grusec & Goodnow, 1994). Based on these theoretical assumptions, this study compared Asian and White American adolescents on three internalization factors (i.e., perceived competence, parental autonomy support, and provision of structure). Results indicate that Asian American students perceive themselves to be more competent than White American adolescents when engaged in studying, worklike activities, and activities important to future goals. Higher levels of perceived competence in these situations appear to make it easier for Asian American adolescents to internalize their cultural values of hard work, respect for education, and high expectations for achievement.

Other studies provide support for this conclusion. Harter (1992), for example, showed that positive affect accompanied by high perceived competence in a given situation promotes a student's internalized motives. Asakawa and Csikszentmihalyi (1998a, 1998b) also reported that Asian American adolescents have significantly more positive experiences (i.e., happier and more enjoyable) than White American adolescents when engaged in studying, worklike activities, and activities important to future goals. Asian Americans' high perceived competence, together with their relatively positive experiences when engaged in the three types of activities, may be conducive to enhancing internalization of relevant cultural values.

When the two new variables of autonomy and structure were used to examine how families from different backgrounds employed these practices, results indicated that Asian American parents were more likely to provide their children with freedom in actual academic activities and structure or guidance for academic success than their White American counterparts. These Asian American parental practices also appeared to be favorable in promoting internalization of values concerned with education.

However, these academic socialization practices seemed to be peculiar to Asian American parents in comparison to practices used by White American parents and parents from intact families. That is, the Asian Americans' parental practices appear to be a balanced combination of freedom and control on different levels of parental involvement. Asian American parents were more likely to provide their children with freedom in actual academic activities than were White American parents. Interestingly, however, parents from intact families were less likely to provide their children with freedom in these activities. In other words, they were more likely to control their children's actual academic activities than their counterparts. Parents who had younger children were also more likely to control their children's actual academic activities. Thus, autonomy support in actual academic activities, which was constructed with Asian Americans' parental practices, may be called permissiveness within mainstream American culture. However, parents from intact families, parents of Asian origin, and parents who had younger children were more likely to provide their children with structure and guidance for academic success than their counterparts.

These findings clearly indicate that the parenting practices of Asian American parents are somewhat different from those of parents from other types of families. More specifically, parents of intact families and young children were more likely to be involved in their children's academic matters at two different levels—microinvolvement, such as checking homework, helping with homework, and discussing things studied in class (controlling children's actual academic activities), and macroinvolvement, such as deciding whether children should go to college, limiting TV time, and discussing standardized test plans and preparation (provision of structure for academic success). In contrast, Asian American parents appeared to take distinct approaches at the different levels of involvement. At the microlevel, Asian American parents provided more freedom, and at the macrolevel they showed more control over their children's lives.

The regression analyses further suggest that the two culturally different groups had somewhat different mechanisms for promoting children's high academic performance. Two factors for promoting the process of internalization (i.e., parents' autonomy support and students' perceived competence while studying) had positive net effects on Asian Americans' school grades. This finding is interesting because Asian Americans' parental autonomy support in actual academic activities positively predicted Asian American students' school performance. However, the same factors were not significant predictors of White American adolescents' school grades.

The same regression analyses also provide us with results to support a differential approach to enhancing students' performance through cultural sensitivity. For White American adolescents, their own attitudes, such as their educational aspirations and sense of control, had strong positive effects on their school performance. However, for Asian Americans, although children's own educational aspirations were also a fair predictor for their school performance, more important, parents' educational expectations and autonomy support had relatively strong effects on students' school grades. In other words, if Asian American parents had higher academic expectations for their children but did not get overly involved in actual academic activities, their children appeared to perform quite well in school. Thus, Asian American parents' attitudes seemed to have relatively strong effects on their adolescents' school performance, whereas White American adolescents' grades depended mostly on their own academic aspirations.

Moreover, these findings appear to reflect the differential interpretations of the self the two culturally diverse groups have. That is, academic performance of Asian American adolescents, who are more likely to have interdependent selves, is affected by parental attitudes and support, whereas the academic achievement of White American adolescents, who are more likely to have independent selves, is promoted mostly by their own educational aspirations and perceived locus of control. Previous research has suggested that academic motivation in an interdependent cultural context may have different aspects from that in an independent context. It has been reported that achievement motivation in Asian cultures is socially oriented (Yang, 1982), is positively correlated with familialism and filial piety (Yu, 1974), and has social or collective origins (Maehr & Nicholls, 1980). It seems that achievement in an interdependent context is motivated by a desire to meet the expectations of others. Those with interdependent selves strive for academic excellence not to achieve separateness or uniqueness, as is assumed for those with independent selves, but to more fully realize their connectedness or interdependence.

It is important to note that the internalization mechanisms examined in this study were unrepresentative of White American adolescents. One explanation is that academic socialization practices of Asian American parents may not be the most effective means for White Americans to promote internalization of their educational values. As cultural psychology suggests, American culture, for the most part, emphasizes independence from others by attending to the individual and his or her unique inner attributes (Markus & Kitayama, 1991). One of the most important values for students in American culture is to become an independent and unique individual. Thus, children's own academic aspirations play an important role in their academic success.

The findings of this study indicated that two factors for promoting the process of internalization of values (i.e., parents' autonomy support and students' perceived competence while studying) appeared to be favorable for Asian Americans to internalize their cultural values relevant to education and academic success. Moreover, these internalization factors actually enhanced Asian American adolescents' school performance. However, for White Americans, the same internalization factors did not appear to have substantial effects on adolescents' self-reported grades. Regarding academic socialization practices, Asian and White American parents took quite different approaches from each other. It seems that the mechanism of internalization of educational values examined in this study is not the typical means for White Americans to promote their children's academic excellence. These differences in academic socialization practices between Asian American and White American groups appear to be a reflection of the cultural imperatives these two culturally different groups stand on.

Asian American parents showed unique parental practices for their children's academic development in comparison to their White American counterparts. From the perspective of Western parenting concepts, the Asian Americans' parental practices may be interpreted as indicating that the parents are not interested or involved in their children's education. However, their practices had substantial effects on their children's school performance. White American children's educational aspirations and serious attitudes toward academics are more likely to develop based on the personal interests that result from their independence. The findings of this study appear to lend support to different models of parental influence on children's academic development. In other words, sending mixed messages may be harmful, but if there is a consistency between philosophy and practice,

then internalization of cultural values is more likely to occur and have its desired effects.

References

Alva, S. A. (1993). Differential patterns of achievement among Asian-American adolescents. *Journal of Youth and Adolescence, 22*, 407–423.

Asakawa, K., & Csikszentmihalyi, M. (1998a). The quality of experience of Asian American adolescents in academic activities: An exploration of educational achievement. *Journal of Research on Adolescence, 8*, 241–262.

Asakawa, K., & Csikszentmihalyi, M. (1998b). The quality of experience of Asian American adolescents in activities related to future goals. *Journal of Youth and Adolescence, 27*, 141–163.

Asakawa, K., & Csikszentmihalyi, M. (2000). Feelings of connectedness and internalization of values in Asian American adolescents. *Journal of Youth and Adolescence, 29*, 121–145.

Baumrind, D. (1971). Current patterns of parental authority. *Developmental Psychology Monographs, 4*, 1–103.

Chao, R. K. (1994). Beyond parental control and authoritarian parenting style: Understanding Chinese parenting through the cultural notion of training. *Child Development, 65*, 1111–1119.

College Board. (1989). *College-bound seniors: 1989 SAT profile.* New York: Author.

Csikszentmihalyi, M., & Schneider, B. (2000). *Becoming adult: How teenagers prepare for the world of work.* New York: Basic Books.

Deci, E. L., & Ryan, R. M. (1985). *Intrinsic motivation and self-determination in human behavior.* New York: Plenum.

Dornbusch, S. M., Ritter, P. L., Leiderman, P. H., Roberts, D. F., & Fraleigh, M. J. (1987). The relation of parenting style to adolescent school performance. *Child Development, 58*, 1244–1257.

Grusec, J. E., & Goodnow, J. J. (1994). Impact of parental discipline methods on the child's internalization of values: A reconceptualization of current points of view. *Developmental Psychology, 30*, 4–19.

Harter, S. (1992). The relationship between perceived competence, affect, and motivational orientation within the classroom: Processes and patterns of change. In A. K. Boggiano & T. S. Pittman (Eds.), *Achievement and motivation: A social-developmental perspective* (pp. 77–114). Cambridge, England: Cambridge University Press.

Herrnstein, R., & Murray, C. (1994). *The bell curve: Intelligence and class structure in American life.* New York: Free Press.

Hirschman, C., & Wong, M. G. (1984). Socioeconomic gains of Asian Americans, Blacks, and Hispanics: 1960–1976. *American Journal of Sociology, 90*, 584–607.

Hirschman, C., & Wong, M. G. (1986). The extraordinary educational attainment of Asian Americans: A search for historical evidence and explanations. *Social Forces, 65*, 1–27.

Hurh, W. M., & Kim, K. C. (1989). The "success" image of Asian Americans: Its validity and its practical and theoretical implications. *Ethnic and Racial Studies, 12*, 512–538.

Ima, K., & Rumbaut, R. G. (1989). Southeast Asian refugees in American schools: A comparison of fluent-English-proficient and limited-English-proficient students. *Topics in Language Disorder, 9*, 54–75.

Jensen, A., & Inouya, A. (1980). Level 1 and level 2 abilities in Asian, white, and black children. *Intelligence, 4*, 41–49.

Kitano, M. K. (1984). Early education for Asian-American children. In O. N. Saracho & B. Spodek (Eds.), *Understanding the multicultural experience in early childhood education* (pp. 45–66). Washington, DC: National Association for the Education of Young Children.

Lee, S. J. (1994). Behind the model-minority stereotype: Voices of high- and low-achieving Asian American students. *Anthropology & Education Quarterly, 25,* 413–429.

Lynn, R., & Dziobon, J. (1980). On the intelligence of Japanese and other Mongoloid peoples. *Personality and Individual Differences, 1,* 95–96.

Maehr, M., & Nicholls, J. (1980). Culture and achievement motivation: A second look. In N. Warren (Ed.), *Studies in cross-cultural psychology* (pp. 221–267). New York: Academic.

Markus, H. R., & Kitayama, S. (1991). Culture and self: Implications for cognition, emotion, and motivation. *Psychological Review, 98,* 224–253.

Mordkowitz, E. R., & Ginsburg, H. P. (1987). Early academic socialization of successful Asian-American college students. *The Quarterly Newsletter of the Laboratory of Comparative Human Cognition, 9,* 285–291.

Ogbu, J. (1983). Minority status and schooling in plural societies. *Comparative Education Review, 27,* 168–190.

Ogbu, J. (1987). Variability in minority school performance: A problem in search of an explanation. *Anthropology & Education Quarterly, 18,* 312–334.

Ogbu, J. (1991). Minority coping responses and school experience. *Journal of Psychohistory, 18,* 433–456.

Ryan, R. M. (1991). The nature of the self in autonomy and relatedness. In J. Strauss & G. R. Goethals (Eds.), *The self: Interdisciplinary approaches* (pp. 208–238). New York: Springer-Verlag.

Ryan, R. M., Connell, J. P., & Grolnick, W. S. (1992). When achievement is not intrinsically motivated: A theory and assessment of self-regulation in school. In A. K. Boggiano & T. S. Pittman (Eds.), *Achievement and motivation: A social-developmental perspective* (pp. 167–188). Cambridge, England: Cambridge University Press.

Ryan, R. M., & Powelson, C. L. (1991). Autonomy and relatedness as fundamental to motivation and education. *Journal of Experimental Education, 60,* 49–66.

Schneider, B., Hieshima, J. A., Lee, S., & Plank, S. (1992). East-Asian academic success in the United States: Family, school, and community explanation. In P. M. Greenfield & R. R. Cocking (Eds.), *Cross-cultural roots of minority child development* (pp. 323–350). Hillsdale, NJ: Lawrence Erlbaum Associates, Inc.

Schneider, B., & Lee, Y. (1990). A model for academic success: The school and home environment of East Asian students. *Anthropology & Education Quarterly, 21,* 358–377.

Shoho, A. R. (1994). A historical comparison of parental involvement of three generations of Japanese Americans (Isseis, Niseis, and Sanseis) in the education of their children. *Journal of Applied Developmental Psychology, 15,* 305–311.

Steinberg, L., Dornbusch, S. M., & Brown, B. B. (1992). Ethnic differences in adolescent achievement: An ecological perspective. *American Psychologist, 47,* 723–729.

Sue, S., & Kitano, H. H. L. (1973). Stereotypes as a measure of success. *Journal of Social Issues, 29,* 83–98.

Sue, S., & Okazaki, S. (1990). Asian-American educational achievements: A phenomenon in search of an explanation. *American Psychologist, 45,* 913–920.

Suzuki, R. H. (1977). Education and the socialization of Asian Americans: A revisionist analysis of the "model minority" thesis. *Amerasia Journal, 4,* 23–52.

Takaki, R. (1989). *Strangers from a different shore: A history of Asian-Americans.* New York: Penguin.

Vernon, P. E. (1982). *The abilities and achievements of Orientals in North America.* New York: Academic.

Wong, M. G., & Hirschman, C. (1983). Labor force participation and socioeconomic attainment of Asian American women. *Sociological Perspective, 26*(4), 3–46.

Yang, K. S. (1982). Causal attributions of academic success and failure and their affective consequences. *Chinese Journal of Psychology, 24,* 65–83.

Yu, E. S. H. (1974). Achievement motive, familism, and hsiao: A replication of McClelland–Winterbottom studies. *Dissertation Abstracts International, 35,* 593A.

Received December 22, 1999
Final revision received August 2, 2000
Accepted September 29, 2000

*For Product Safety Concerns and Information please contact
our EU representative GPSR@taylorandfrancis.com Taylor & Francis
Verlag GmbH, Kaufingerstraße 24, 80331 München, Germany*

T - #0205 - 270225 - C0 - 297/210/4 - PB - 9780805897197 - Gloss Lamination